you are
not alone

you are not alone

not alone

A new way to grieve

CARIAD LLOYD

TONIC

LONDON · OXFORD · NEW YORK · NEW DELHI · SYDNEY

BLOOMSBURY TONIC
Bloomsbury Publishing Plc
50 Bedford Square, London, WC1B 3DP, UK
29 Earlsfort Terrace, Dublin 2, Ireland

BLOOMSBURY is a trademark of Bloomsbury Publishing Plc

First published in Great Britain, 2023

A catalogue record for this book is available from the British Library

ISBN: HB: 978-1-5266-2183-2; TPB: 978-1-5266-2184-9;
eBook: 978-1-5266-2185-6; ePDF: 978-1-5266-4640-8

2 4 6 8 10 9 7 5 3 1

Typeset by Newgen KnowledgeWorks Pvt. Ltd., Chennai, India
Printed and bound in Great Britain by CPI Group (UK) Ltd, Croydon CR0 4YY

To find out more about our authors and books visit www.bloomsbury.com
and sign up for our newsletters

'Death is not an event in life: we do not live to experience death. If we take eternity to mean not infinite temporal duration but timelessness, then eternal life belongs to those who live in the present. Our life has no end in the way in which our visual field has no limits.'

Ludwig Wittgenstein

'Wow! That is the real McCoy!'

My dad, when eating a particularly good curry

To Dad,
Thank you for answering my questions, embarrassing me, and for
telling me endlessly I could do anything I put my mind to.

To Mum,
Thank you. For <u>everything</u>.

Hello,
Welcome to the club.
I'm sorry you're here.
I know you didn't ask to be here.

You didn't know grief felt like this.
It isn't fair. It's awful.
Deeply, truly hideously, awful.

You didn't know it would feel like this.
Now they're dead. Everything has changed.
Everything.
The world isn't the same.
Everything you knew and loved is irrevocably changed.
I'm sorry.

It's a really shit club.
You don't get told when you're going to enter it.
Some people get no warning at all.
There's no reward scheme or discounts.
(There should be: if you have two deaths in one year,
you should get free parking or a voucher, at least.)
The club is full of loss and pain and sadness and anger
and fear, and in the middle, is a great big empty hole.

They should be here.
And they're not.
There are other people in the club,
There are so many of us.

I know you feel alone. But we're here.
We know grief. Not yours. Yours is your own and no one else knows it or carries it.
Sometimes bits of all the grief-mess look the same, sometimes they don't.
But I know how hard it is to carry. I know how heavy it is.

I got to the club early, so I put out some nibbles (pretzels and crisps).
You're welcome.
(There are dips too, but you don't look that hungry yet.)

I've been in the club for a long time.
I've been carrying my grief-mess for a long time.
When you first join, you can only see the hole in the middle of your soul,
Nothing else.

Then, after a few years,
Your eyes slowly adjust.
And you can see the hole in the middle and the other stuff too.
You can see the other people in the club.
And the outside world.
It's foggy at first, but it's still there.
Trudging on. Existing.
It's still here.
The world is still here.
You're still here.
They are not.

I can't promise you it will be okay.
I can't make it better.
I can just be here with you.
Because,
You are not alone.

Contents

Peter Fraser Lloyd, 1953–1998

The End and the Beginning

I don't really say his name a lot. It can be a bit much. It still hurts to go into the details of who he was – seems easier to just say: 'My dad died when I was fifteen.' A vague enough sentence to leave a sufficient gap between me and his death. A cushion between the words I'm saying and the memories that appear in front of me. That's his name and that's his time on earth and, yes, it aches still to write it down. Still feels raw, even now, to go precisely into detail and not to a protective sentence. 'My dad died when I was fifteen.' The group of words I'm used to carrying, used to saying, so that they have no pain or edges any more.

I come into the living room and sit on the big sofa. He is there, with my mum. He is sat by the bay window on the small, floral, upholstered chair that my mum inherited from someone – designed for a dressing room, not for brutal truths. He isn't really looking at me or leading this. That is unusual. It's daytime, February. Bright but not warm. I am facing them both in our suburban semi-detached house where nothing happens (until today).

He is in front of me. He already looks bad: he's gone yellow, really yellow, like someone has coloured him in with a felt-tip. 'It's jaundice,' they'd said. I'm fifteen, I don't know what jaundice means, and now they've called me in to talk. My mum says he's got cancer. Does she say the pancreas? She must do, I don't remember. I remember feeling sick, looking at my hands and asking to leave. I want to leave the room because I can't take in the words in the air. I can't swallow them down. They are inedible, unbreathable.

I go to my bedroom, slump to the floor (knees don't work well when you're grieving), put my dressing gown in my mouth and sob as quietly as I can. I don't want anyone to know what's happening to me at that moment, why I am sat there. If they had asked what I was doing, I wouldn't have had an answer. I didn't know any more. I wasn't in control any more. I was lost. From this point, I was lost.

This is the beginning of my journey to grief. This is where who I am now began — in February 1998, aged fifteen, living on the edge of London and on the edge of nothing interesting. Quiet, safe, peaceful. My overriding sense of my childhood is summer — green leaves waving softly in the wind, sleepovers, laughter, *Star Wars*, holidays, Findus Crispy Pancakes at teatime on trays in front of the telly, waiting for *Fresh Prince* to come on ...

This is where it changed, and I began.

Introduction

Facts

I'm a long-term member of 'the club'.

DDC* member since 1998 (*Dead Dad Club, subsection: pancreatic cancer; division: teenager when he died; category (ii) – died quickly after diagnosis. Grief Points: 57[1]).

He was diagnosed with secondary pancreatic cancer in February 1998.

Celine Dion's 'My Heart Will Go On' was on the radio everywhere we went.

(It didn't, though, did it.)

On 21 April 1998, he died.

I was fifteen.

I stopped being a teenager.[2]

I became a grown-up in one fell swoop of a tumour no one had known about, but also –

I froze at that moment, the eternal adolescent.

Because to move forward would be to move into a world he didn't know.

---

[1] There aren't really Grief Points, sorry. It's not nearly as good as a Boots Advantage Card.

[2] I wasn't a great one. If you're imagining 'Teenage Kicks' playing while I down a bottle of vodka, change that to one whose only rebellion is to smoke, but mostly prefers watching *Gardeners' World*, followed by *Red Dwarf*, on a wild Friday night.

I learnt what forever meant.

I became full of grief.

So full, I couldn't breathe,

Or think of anything else, some days.

I can chart my life before my dad died and after my dad died.

I can split my life into two, the cut slicing my own narrative.

This is the point where I understood.

Where I joined the club.

He liked to run marathons and triathlons. He was training for an Ironman.

He was a very noisy person; you were always aware he was in the room. Not chatty but one of those people who would cough and breathe and sigh and think LOUDLY.

He liked Jean-Michel Jarre and Frank Zappa.

He was obsessed with correct grammar and if you said, 'Tom and me', he'd correct it to, 'Tom and I'. He did this by saying 'AND I' while you were in the middle of talking.

He used to like watching the Tour de France and opera, and he could clear a lift with his farts.

He's dead, but before that, he was my dad.

Find Your Way

Some days we got on, mostly we didn't. A lot of the time we weren't great at communicating. This isn't a love letter to him from a grieving daughter who never recovered from the loss of her daddy. That's not what happened, that's not who we were. This isn't a book that will tell you how I recovered from a great tragedy. It was sad, but my story isn't tragic, it's depressingly everyday.

This isn't how to solve grief (*In Just 10 Days You Too Can Pretend They're Still Alive!*). At its most scientific, this book is the result of many experiments in grief, my own and those of the many others I have spoken to – comedians, writers, actors, producers; end-of-life doulas, grief psychotherapists, palliative care doctors; people who have suffered the loss of parents, siblings, children, babies, grandparents, pets, friends, partners, pregnancies, wives, husbands; from those who went suddenly with no warning, to those who were taken slowly with too much pain – all of us with grief, all of us trying to find our way through a subject society still struggles to talk about (even though all humans will one day experience it).

This book is the result of all the conversations and information I gathered trying to find my way through my own grief. At its most useful, it's a map. I can't plan your journey, but I can show you (sketched in felt-tip pen on a bit of scrap paper) that this is the route I took. It wasn't easy but I got there, and today I'm okay.

I'm still in the club, even now, all these years later. You don't leave once you've joined; it's a life membership. Grief eases and changes and returns, but it never disappears. If you're searching for an answer to stop it, I can't offer you that and I wouldn't trust anyone who says they can. But it isn't a hopeless quest to find ways to ease your grief – to look at your 'grief-mess' and understand it, to learn how to carry it alongside your life, learn how to hold it in a way that allows you to have joy but also remember that person and acknowledge the sadness. I know at the start of grief it can seem impossible it will ever change: that feeling *is* grief. But like all things, it does change. The depths of futility, of pain, of sadness, are all part of the process. Each grief is unique. I will never fully understand yours, as you will never understand that spring in 1998, but we have all felt the agonising pain and somehow made it through the night.

This map doesn't offer you an exit, just suggestions for how to navigate this new world and help you as you learn grief's brutal but beautiful lesson: that grief will change and grow and diminish and reappear, it will be with you forever. You will learn to build a life around it, to carry it. I know that for some reading this statement it will seem an impossible feat but, hear me from the back of the club, it will be okay. You will be okay. Somehow, you will be.

Though I began this journey at fifteen when my father died, I only began to understand its effects on me after I started my podcast, *Griefcast*, in 2016: talking about death and grief in weekly bursts, just myself and another *griefster*[3] reflecting on our experiences. There I finally opened the box (you know, the box in your mind you've piled all the grief into and closed the lid on because ...). Once I opened it, and the tears didn't drown me, a healing occurred that I didn't know was possible after so many years. I opened my most painful memories and began to share them in a weekly downloadable format.

---

[3] The term actor and writer Robert Webb coined for the members of the club when I spoke to him about his grief on the podcast.

How many people would want to listen anyway, I pondered, to me talking to others about death in a cheery manner? I was convinced that it would be unnoticeable, a small raindrop in a large pond. Then, the first season of just four episodes turned into nine seasons, and slowly over the years into nearly 200 episodes, millions of downloads, multiple awards, hundreds of conversations and thousands of emails from listeners. I say this not to brag, I am still a little stunned. I realised the club wasn't merely full – it was rammed. I wasn't alone, when all this time, all these years, I had thought I was. But we're all here, with differing sizes of mess in our hands – huge, big squiggles of griefs. We know what it's like to carry this and still try to live.

This book is made up of reflections on my grief-mess and everything I've learnt from carrying it for so long. Your grief-mess will look different, but maybe I can help with carrying it for a bit, like a great backpack?[4] We can stand next to each other in the club and know we're both here. What's happened to us isn't unusual, it's normal to know death, to have known it. Grief is normal.

Once I realised how full the club was, my grief-mess became a little lighter. I could see my grief as part of the human process, not something that had happened to me beyond my control. I could see it as part of living; to hold grief was part of the deal of this life. Once I knew there were even others in the pancreatic-cancer-dead-dad room, my pain eased. As I began to talk, other people spoke to

---

[4] Like one with a great laptop pocket, but somehow not too bulky either. Sigh, the dream.

me and we shared stories and pain and laughter, and we remembered our person – and it helped.

This is also my learnt experience from talking to those in the club, people who understood, who wanted to talk about the subject everyone else was avoiding. What unites us is not the cause of death, the length of the illness or the suddenness of the accident. What unites all the grief-messes is that we are still carrying them, holding the pain and the loss. We have all learnt how to carry the grief as best we can, to live our lives alongside it. We are all in the club, still, no matter how short or long our grief journey has been. It isn't easy, or painless, but it's possible. That's what I can offer you: it is possible.

Grief is a huge, swirling, tangled ball of wires – like the worst headphone knot you have ever seen. Unsolvable. You will spend your life untangling it, noticing strands, following them, almost thinking you've smoothed out all the sadness, and then a rush, a pain, a wave of grief will consume you again. We are always at the shore, we can watch as that grief tide goes out so far, but it will come back to us. We can get stronger muscles to hold it, we can sometimes hand it to others for moments of rest, but it is still our grief, it is a part of us. Whatever visual metaphor helps you. I will not lead you through to a world where it doesn't exist. I will ask you the questions that helped me understand my grief, and hopefully lead you to the answers that will make your grief knowable. I will also tell you my story, of how I have learnt to live with it. I will tell you I am happy: I still have my grief-mess, and yet I am happy. Some days it's heavy, some days it's so light that I don't know it's there. It changed me. It made me. I am happy. I am sad. I am okay.[5]

I want you to know that you are not alone with all this pain. I want you to see how many others feel like this. Grief is inevitable, a guaranteed human experience. This is a wish to myself, aged fifteen, and a guide to all the things I didn't know when I became the person-whose-dad-had-died, when I began to be someone who had a grief-mess to hold. I hope it's helpful. I hope it soothes. I hope you're as okay today as can be expected. And I hope you know: you are not alone. There are so many of us here. You are not alone.

---

[5] Perhaps you are reading this and you're not 'in the club'. You may have picked up this book because you want to help someone who is (thank you for that). Perhaps you are heading towards your first Big Grief and want to know what is coming; perhaps you just want to face these things before life forces you to. If you haven't experienced big G grief yet, I know it can be hard to believe that a death, just one death, can split your life in half, into pieces, into tatters. It's not easy to explain to those on the outside that when you love someone and then they die, it breaks your soul (if you're not keen on soul, I just mean your 'you', your heart, your essence, your inner joy that makes everything okay. That's what I mean by soul). A piece of it breaks. You're left with a gap inside you. I can describe it endlessly but until it happens to you, you won't know the exact feeling. Like I can't truly communicate what it feels like to eat a ham and tomato roll from the Victoria Bakery on Barnet High Street. Because it really was perfect. A flawless ratio of ham and fresh tomato in the fluffiest soft white roll, with just a slightly crunchy crust. But the bakery closed down, and so now you need to take my word for how good it was – and how it feels inside the club. If you haven't got here yet, it can be hard to understand how it changes you forever. You can still help those who are trying to find their way to a place that makes sense. You can encourage them to keep going; let them say *their* name and weep and be sad. They will need more time than you both think.

This is a book about death.
This is a book about grief.

This is a book about the mess.
This is a book about the complexities.
This is a book about how you don't get over it.
This is a book about the pain.
This is a book about the loss.
This is a book about how you don't get over it.
This is a book about the weirdness of it all.
This is a book about when you were bored at the hospital.
This is a book about when you howled and wept and sobbed so loudly it sounded like a goose honking which made you laugh out loud, and it stopped your tears.
This is a book about how you don't get over it.
This is a book about how it can affect you, even if you haven't seen them for years.
This is a book about how we don't talk about it.
This is a book about how you don't get over it.
This is a book about how you worried what to wear to the funeral.
This is a book about how you know they waited for you to get there.
This is a book about how you just left the room for a second and they went.
This is a book about how you don't get over it.
This is a book about how there is no right way to do this.
This is a book about letting go of the shame of doing this 'wrong'.

This is a book about death.
This is a book about grief.

This is a book to say again and again:
you are not alone.

There are two strands to this book: the main chapters, which cover the many lessons I have learnt about grief, and the interludes. The interludes are brief vignettes that follow the path of my own grief. Sometimes they're much sadder, so, if you want to avoid a cry, you can come back to them later. Or if you want to dive in for a weep, you can start there.

Chicken Guilt

We are sat on the sofa – mine and mum's sofa. Sometimes you sat with us, but it's not your sofa. The other sofa is my brother's (the place of his favourite game to annoy me – placing the remote on the arm, knowing I can see it but will never be fast enough to grab it back and gain control of the living room).

We are sat together on the sofa – already unusual. You're ill, so you're watching telly with me. A part of you has already given up. You normally can't sit still enough to watch telly, hate trash TV, only sit down for the Tour de France or the *Ring* cycle (I mean, it's not a surprise no one will watch telly with you). You're still yellow. The swish of your shell-suit-style trousers told me you were coming down the hall.

It's post-tea telly time. I am working my way through *The Simpsons* and then on to *Fresh Prince*, a blissful hour of no thoughts. In front of me on the coffee table is my tray with the end of my tea (I've had roast chicken leg and tinned sweetcorn – my mum is a fan of things that you can heat up quickly). You sit down next to me, at the other end of the sofa. My legs are curled up so you can't get too near. You ask me to take my tray out to the kitchen (the plastic trays mum serves tea on. My brother's tray is striped, mine has a twee forest scene on it – hedgehogs and rabbits in the leaves. I'll smash this tray later, when you're dead, but today it holds a plate of bones, gravy and scraps).

'I'll do it in a minute,' I say.

I mean it. I will. I'm tired and fifteen and watching something. I don't mind you being there but it's still weird.

'Take your tray out please.' [Irritated now.]

'Oh, here we go,' I think. I've told him I'll do it in a minute.

'Yeah,' I say.

I mean, for fuck's sake, I will. I'm not swearing at him at the moment (now he has cancer). He huffs and shifts on the sofa. He's ruining the programme. What does he want? Why is he being so huffy?

I zone back in. Bart or Lisa or Carlton, someone far away from my world, is talking, making me laugh.

He breaks, shouts as only he can, a sudden sonic boom: 'Take your tray out, it's making me feel sick!'

I feel sick.

My stomach fills with bile, my cheeks go red. I leap up and take it to the kitchen. I'm shaking. Tears are filling my eyes (these are the early days of not knowing how to swallow them so that no one knows). I run upstairs. I sob and sob and sob and sob.

Why didn't I take it? Why didn't I do as I was told? Why didn't he say? I'm furious and sobbing. I didn't know. I didn't know. I didn't know.

The endless refrain of February to April 1998: I didn't know. I didn't understand. I didn't −

For years this is an example of my *pure selfishness*. How I let him down, how unthinking I was. I didn't know. I realise years later — I didn't know. I just didn't understand. What chemo meant, what this mysterious, dark-haired, brown-eyed man who lived with us was feeling. I didn't really understand him before he was ill, and when someone gets cancer that doesn't magically change. We didn't have time to explain it to each other. I'm sorry, I didn't know. I know you knew that. Two tired family members trying to figure out what death means in front of Will Smith and chicken bones.

Sorry.

21 April 1998 – The End

It was over twenty years ago now, so the memories are not fresh. They are faded, but the shadow of the scar remains. The day of his death can't be described here in vivid, traumatic detail. I am grasping to remember a nightmare I had when I was fifteen. Telling you what the cover of my German textbook looked like that year would be hard, despite having it in my life longer than my dad's cancer, so please excuse the blurry edges to this memory.

I didn't want to go to the hospital that morning. We had been every day that week to see him. They moved him into the cancer ward of Mount Vernon Hospital, too sick to get to the hospice they said. It was somewhere near Watford I think – even now I still don't know or want to pin it down too precisely for fear of adding more reality to it. I know we drove north. I know it was the year *Titanic* came out. I know I heard 'My Heart Will Go On' a lot on drives to the hospital. I know I thought it was funny – that Celine would sing about her heart going on and here we were watching a body die. It seemed as if Celine Dion did really want my dad to be okay; it seemed funny to me that we would have to listen to it on car journeys back and forth to see him. Like a really good gag the Fates had written for me.

I didn't want to go in on 20 April. I sat on the sofa and asked my mum to let me have the day off from a visit. She was sitting in the chair, the flowery and valanced one that belonged in a boudoir, like she was speaking to me from the past – the front garden growing and living through the window behind her, full of green bushes and spring flowers. She said, 'I think you should come in today.' I didn't ask any more questions after that because I was too terrified. It's easy to forget that teenage sullenness can actually be translated as: 'I have no idea what's happening and I'm hoping if I stay silent you might explain it more.'

We drove there. Celine was really hopeful again (thanks Celine). We drove in a red car to the red-brick, crumbling hospital surrounded by large trees covered in leaves. Everywhere seemed in spring, in life, apart from us. My brother and I sat in the hospital café: a huge, vaulted room with high ceilings, like a temple to baked beans on toast and cold steel cutlery, eating our sad teas.

There was a procession of family and close friends to his ward room; we stayed as they said their goodbyes. I know we waited all night. I know I slept on the floor by his bed in the small private room he'd been given so he could die in it. I know the sun rose and I know my mum begged him to go into the light, to stop fighting. 'Go Pete,' she said, again and again, 'go into the light.' She held his hand and told him to let it happen because it already had. I know we were all round his bedside and I know he died at 9.40 a.m. on 21 April because, as it happened, I noted it – the time, the date. The same day, but not month, of my birthday. Just noted it; didn't feel much else. Funny, I thought, the Fates back with more jokes.

I went into the room after the nurses had sorted him, tidied him into his peaceful-death position. Pyjamas on, tubes gone, clean white pillow. I looked at his face, his now dead face. A dead body, a dead face, dead eyes, and dead hands neatly clasped on top of his chest. He didn't look like my dad any more. Because he wasn't moving, eating noisily, breathing or sniffing. My dad was an alive man. A man who lived and it echoed out of him through noise, smells and sounds. But now he was very still. There was no life in this person. He was gone. He was dead. This was just a body now. I realised he had been something else, the energy that drove the physical. That energy had gone. He was dead. Ah Lord, he was gone, what the fuck happens now? I know I opened the French windows in his room. They opened onto a grubby patio that needed repaving – broken slabs and an attempt at pot plants. I opened them because I wanted him to be able to go, to finally leave. Wherever he needed to go, I wanted him to be able to go there now.

I

The End
(of the Linear Narrative)

What Should Grief Feel Like?

You're here. You enter the first room of the club with your raging grief-mess (a constantly moving squiggle, like some cartoon fight, arms and legs flying out of a cloud of emotion). You enter this new world with them gone. You are only carrying your grief and your expectations. Because, aware of it or not, you've been holding preconceived ideas of what grief should look and feel like, ideas you barely even noticed you've been absorbing. And now here you are, with your most terrible fears realised and your grief wrapping itself around you.

This is going to be a long journey. We aren't looking to fix this mess or throw it away. We're looking to learn to carry it. But how can we learn to carry it lightly? Will there be a day when it doesn't feel so heavy, so hard, so painful?[1]

To begin the process of being able to hold our grief-mess more easily, we need to unpick what our current conceptions of grief are. First, it can be helpful to examine our guilt. You may be here because you think you have done something 'wrong' thus far with your grief. You may be examining your behaviour before or after the death and finding it odd, troubling, too emotional, not emotional enough. I want to look at where this idea of 'good grief' comes from. What have you been told is the right way to do grief? What were your preconceived ideas of what this

---

[1] Just to answer this now, in case that's all you want to know: it is not an overnight process; it's a slow, steady one – think of moss taking over a rock, creating a soft bed for your thoughts and heart.

process would look like? Let's start at the beginning ... where grief began.

I'm being silly of course. Grief never 'began', it's always been with us. To live is ... to die. The act of burying the dead is one of the oldest human traditions, presumably growing out of the need to give death a ritual (and also, I guess, to stop spreading whatever disease Ug the Caveperson died of). Death is as old as Time – and Grief is their cat, one of those mega old ones you thought had died but is still sitting in the corner hacking up a furball. I'm still being silly, but the point remains. You can't live without dying, you can't live without grief eventually finding you.

For a lot of us, the concept of what grief should feel like begins with Elisabeth Kübler-Ross's 1969 book, *On Death and Dying*. None of those words may be familiar to you, but what you're likely to be familiar with is the theory this book set in motion: the Five Stages model of grief. That theory has a cultural weight as heavy as the Beatles or *The Godfather* – it's in our modern psyche. You may not have read *On Death and Dying* but you will probably be aware of its central premise: the idea that grief has five stages, and that these stages will lead you through pain and on through to acceptance. You may not even have recalled this theory until you found yourself in grief and began to search for an answer to make it stop.

You are not alone in hoping for it to stop. You are not wrong to think this. You are not foolish to have imagined there is a road to walk down that makes sense. For YEARS that is what we have been told, over and over again. To this day people meet grief for the first time and are handed the idea that if they follow a certain path – successfully move through the Five Stages – they will reach 'The End'.

23

THIS IS NOT TRUE.
THIS IS A LIE.
WELCOME TO THE NEW WORLD.
IT'S SAD AND PAINFUL BUT IF YOU STOP
LOOKING FOR AN END IT'S MUCH EASIER.
I'M NOT SHOUTING. OKAY, SORRY I AM, A BIT
— *I'll step back.*

I want to be clear, because people still think that the Five Stages is real. It is still put forward as an effective way of dealing with grief, and I, very strongly,[2] don't think it is.

Now, I'm not a grief expert, a psychologist, a psycho-therapist, a counsellor or even a confident swimmer. So, before I rip apart the most famous theory on grief without any qualifications to do so (besides my 57 Grief Points — let's not forget them), I want to explain why it makes me so f***ing rageful that the Five Stages is still (ironically) alive today. Because you may have noticed that I am little bit angry about the Five Stages of grief model, and a large part of this fury comes from how the theory made *me* feel all those years ago.

Before my dad died, before I joined the club, I had heard of the Five Stages of grief. I was aware of it, I had unknowingly consumed it, and it sat there ready to be pulled out when it was needed. I vaguely knew that it was about denial, anger and some other stuff. It was a list of the emotions you'd go through when you experienced a death. It was very sad but then, thankfully, at the end, you felt better — you were done. I didn't read this anywhere, I just knew it.

---

[2] You'd never know.

(Like I knew that when people got cancer, they looked a bit pale, said wise things and would die, peacefully, by closing their eyes.) I heard people mention the stages of grief when someone had died. I saw it in films, in TV programmes. I knew confidently that after death there was a process, a nice straight line to follow – a sequence of emotions to tick off and an end goal to head towards. That's great to know. Not so bad. *Phew, grief is gonna be easy!*

So, if someone was still sad after a death, perhaps they weren't working through it properly, they hadn't read the instructions correctly, or they weren't doing it right? Sounds like maybe they were choosing to be sad about it. Maybe they weren't trying hard enough to get through the stages? Maybe they didn't really want to be happy? All perfectly reasonable assumptions if you believe that the Five Stages of grief model holds the truth.

1998. My Dad Dies

Grief begins, suddenly, violently, horrifically. My world is turned upside down, spun in a washing machine, chucked about and stomped on. I am in shock. I am furious. I am also heartbroken and … I don't feel one thing, or rather, I feel too many things: a rush of a thousand emotions that are so loud and so raw it is impossible to identify them individually. All I know is I'm FEELING. Not sure what, but it's definitely emotions – and not the fun ones. It's pretty fucking awful. I am only fifteen, so I haven't experienced shock and trauma at this level, ever. I haven't really been depressed or even that sad (I realise now). I know how I feel is bad. I know it's not nice. I know I am not happy.

I search for a map, the Five Stages magical map, to get me out of these FEELINGS. I am looking for something to slow it down, to isolate individual emotions, to even know what it is I am feeling so strongly. But, as I try to pin down what direction I should be going in, as I read more about the Five Stages, it doesn't make sense to me. I am on the right map. He's definitely dead. I can see my blue dot – there I am surrounded by the pale blue circle of grief – but there doesn't seem to be any way out. There isn't a path to anywhere that isn't grief. My blue dot seems to be facing the wrong way – or occasionally it's floating and sometimes it's not where I thought it was. I must be doing something wrong. I think I'm supposed to be at a stage. Where are they? I'm supposed to work my way through them: starter, main, then pudding. I want to get to pudding. Stage 1: Denial? – What was that? Did I do that? He *was* dead; I wasn't saying he wasn't dead. Stage 3: Bargaining? – With who? He's dead now.

None of it made sense to me, this impossible checklist. How could I finish it if I hadn't started it properly? How could I get to this magical land of Acceptance if I hadn't completed all the levels? I hadn't even beaten the big boss on level Anger yet. How many gold coins did I have to collect before I could leave Depression?

A few months into my grief, after the initial shock faded, things began to settle. My ears adjusted to the cacophony of FEELINGS, and one floated to the top: Anger. Of course, it did, because my anger was *so* angry that it punched the other feelings out of the way. Anger, great: I knew this was a stage, so that's good, that's part of the checklist. But, hmm, I noticed, I'm not moving through it. I'm just angry. All the time.

I seemed to be stuck. I knew you were allowed some anger, but then you were supposed to be done with all your anger and move on to the next bit. This wasn't happening to me. I was just angry. Occasionally sadness crept in, but anger rose louder and suffocated the sadness so that all that came out of my mouth was shouting. This felt very wrong. My mum wasn't as furious as I was; she seemed numb. My brother was angry at first, then resigned to it all. No one else was carrying around a hot ball of burning molten lava inside their stomach. Carefully holding it, in place of their intestines. A rage so frightening that it controlled me. It decided how I felt, it was the only FEELING now.

People didn't like it. My family didn't like it, my teachers didn't like it, my friends weren't that keen. So, I began to feel ashamed of how I was dealing with this grief. How embarrassing to have only one emotion about such an important event in my life. I must be really screwing up this grief thing, I must be doing it really wrong. And guess what ... that made me feel angrier and more ashamed. Because I knew, thanks to the Five Stages, that I couldn't get to 'The End' if I was stuck here, I couldn't get to Acceptance. I couldn't get to feeling better again.

Now, with the calming balm of time (like milk after chillies), I can see what the anger was doing. It was building a fortress of fury to protect me from being sad. To protect me from being vulnerable. No one wants to help/talk to/rescue angry people, which is exactly what I wanted: to be left alone. It gave me a moment to let my brain catch up with reality. He's dead. He died. That's what's happened. He's gone.

If you have felt THE ANGER, then you have felt *the guilt* too. I want you to know it's okay to be angry about death. It's not a stage to pass through. It's a feeling that is valid in your grief – whenever it happens. I would like to go back and apologise to Cariad the teenager and tell her to stop feeling bad about the fury. I felt terribly guilty because the grief culture I'd absorbed told me that this wasn't what grief looked like. Grief in films was an explosion before relief, a punch to the wall and then into tears – a place you passed through. I wasn't softening, I was hardening.

Feeling guilty about it is another way to berate yourself and ignore the sadness. Now I can see my anger wasn't a stage to be passed through. It was valid, it was allowed, it was how I was grieving and what I needed to do at the time. But I didn't know that then.

So many of us don't know we are allowed to grieve in a messy unstructured way because of the shadow of the Five Stages. If you are furious, it's not 'wrong', because there isn't a 'right'. You haven't failed the grief exam, you shouldn't be 'over it'. You are allowed to FEEL – because someone has DIED. And that might mean lots of swearing. I wish someone had given me permission to grieve, however I was grieving. To be messy and angry and sad and afraid. I give you permission now. You can grieve however you fucking like.[3]

Grief is not a straight path.
Grief is not a board game you finish.
Grief is a mess you carry forever.

As I left my rage behind, many, many years later (after many, many therapy sessions), I became an anti-Five Stage

---

[3] Obvs no hurting yourself or others; easy on the mind-altering substances; as much Netflix as you like IMO.

zealot. I wanted to shout loudly about its flaws because I knew the harm it had done to me. I hoped that young people now would not turn to it, that we had moved on from where I was in 1998. After all, the internet exists, you can google your way out of the gravitational pull of the Five Stages. So I had hoped.

A few years after starting my podcast I was at a grief event (yes, a grief event. It's not all tears and wailing, sometimes we meet up[4]) aimed specifically at young grievers. The other members of the panel and I had spoken about our personal experiences and generally it had been an excellent night of honest 'death chat'.[5] As I was leaving, a person came up to me, a cool, young twenty-something Londoner person. She said she'd been too shy to ask a question in front of everyone but she wanted to ask me something privately. Her twin sister had died a few months ago and she was worried that she wasn't grieving correctly. She was worrying because she didn't seem to be going through the Five Stages of grief like she knew she was meant to. In fact, she didn't know how to do the stages. Did I have any advice? She asked me what I thought she was doing wrong.

F*** OFF FIVE STAGES

is what happened inside my head. Here it was again. I felt like shaking my fist in the air, 'Damn you Five Stages! Must you haunt me so!'

---

[4] Quite a bit of tears and wailing, to be fair.
[5] It was organised by the Grief Network, an excellent community who set up events in real life and online to help young grievers connect with others in their position. More information is available in the resources section at the back of this book.

Here she was, just a few months into debilitating grief – just as I had been twenty years before – staring at the empty map, scared she'd already gone wrong. The lie was still winning, it was still out there. Even now in the land of podcasts and #grief, the first thing she had stumbled upon had made her feel as though she was doing something wrong.

You <u>cannot</u> do grief wrong.

From now – immediately – you can stop thinking there is a correct way to do grief. There isn't. I want us to let go of this false idea forever. Let go of the idea that grief has a linear narrative, check-points to tick off as you go, a shopping list to work your way down. Let go that it can be completed, that it can be finished, that it can be done. That if you travel through five distinct isolated emotions you will come through to a place of no pain and no grief. This is what I said to her. I explained that the Five Stages is an outdated idea which can be restricting, and that the original theory has been *misinterpreted*.

She looked at me a little shocked. She glanced away, took a deep breath, and then looked back at me. 'Really?' she asked again. She seemed a little stunned. No one had told her that; no one had released her from the Five Stages headlock.

THERE'S NO RIGHT WAY TO GRIEVE.

That's why I shout. That's why I use caps. Because people still turn to the Five Stages, despite its ancientness. We aren't rattling around eating food left over from 1969, so please can we stop consuming this old theory that is unhelpful to grievers. It's harmful. It hurts the grieving to believe in it. The young woman at the event looked at me again, relief on her face. 'Oh,' she said. 'That's why I can't do it!' She laughed. We both did. (Then we did a little bit of crying, because it was a grief event.)

Isn't it a mad idea – that someone figured how to make this complicated, messy and human process into a board game you could finish – isn't that just hilarious really? I gave her a hug (ahh, pre-Covid). I felt such comfort that she knew the truth because, when you are lost in grief, the idea that there is a way to get out of it that you are not managing to achieve is, hellish.

YOU ARE NOT DOING IT WRONG.
THERE IS NO RIGHT WAY TO GRIEVE.
(Just to be clear.)

The staying power that the Five Stages grief model possesses is strangely admirable. Like a really good earworm, it has been humming away in the background for a very long time. You know it, you've been made aware of it, you very much hope it's true. So, what really is the Five Stages model beyond the vague idea that we've inherited?

The Five Stages of grief is the theory that after you experience a death, you flow through five different emotional states before finally reaching an acceptance of your loss. It has become a cultural touchstone that people (often not in the club) return to again and again. And this is the tragedy of the Five Stages model, because this is not what the Five Stages claims. Elisabeth Kübler-Ross first presented her theory in her book, *On Death and Dying*. She did not write a book called *Five Stages to Pass Through Before You Never Feel Grief Again!* This is just the incredibly powerful and seductive idea that we have been captivated by. We have cherry-picked her theory to make it work for what we WISH was true.

Allow me to introduce you formally to the Five Stages of grief theory: meet Denial, Anger, Bargaining, Depression and Acceptance. The worst boy band ever made. Before we dissect what Kübler-Ross was writing, I want to point out the context in which her theory was framed, and what an amazing woman she was.

Things that are helpful to know before you slag off Kübler-Ross:

1. She was a Swiss-American psychiatrist.
2. She was the recipient of nineteen honorary degrees.
3. In 1965 she became assistant professor of psychiatry at the University of Chicago and conducted a series of interviews with terminal patients.
4. It is from this work, of interviewing people with terminal illnesses, that she developed the Five Stages model – five stages that, in general, an individual experiences when facing their *imminent death*.
5. She helped to forge the hospice movement, believing that the dying deserved a peaceful place to be able to accept death.
6. In 1985 she tried to build a hospice for infants and children diagnosed with HIV but was stopped from doing so by local West Virginia residents who believed they would be infected by the virus.

7. She wrote more than twenty books about death and helping the dying.
8. She also got involved with a psychic channeller, who was then exposed as a fraud and involved in unlawful sexual activities. (But that was in 1976 in California, and I imagine it was hard *not* to get involved with a psychic channeller involved in unlawful sexual activities then.)

On Death and Dying is an incredible book – for its time. It genuinely helped change the conversation around death and the rights of dying patients. One of Kübler-Ross's main evaluations was that patients should be told they are dying. Through her work as a psychotherapist, she came to realise that doctors were not informing patients that they were in hospital because they were about to die.

It's hard to imagine quite how different 1969 was to now, because miniskirts still make sense, but a lot of the other stuff was draconian lunacy. Kübler-Ross writes eloquently about the doctors and nurses she worked with at the time, and how their own fear of death caused them to shield patients from the truth, causing more harm to the patients – acts of protection turning into acts of harm. The language employed was also problematic. They struggled to describe to the sick what it was they were dying from. There weren't specifics, you couldn't understand the nuances of your type of bowel cancer, for example: the term 'malignancy' was used as a catch-all word for cancers, end of the discussion. Sometimes a wife might be advised or a husband half-informed that 'it's serious', or parents told that their child was 'very sick'. The patients themselves, however, were not informed.

Medical professionals believed that the person who was sick and about to die would not be able to cope with the knowledge that they were, in fact, dying.

In America in the late 1960s, hospitals were full of patients in agony taking medicines and undergoing painful procedures that they believed would eventually make them better. They weren't told that most of these treatments would not ultimately work. In *On Death and Dying* Kübler-Ross suggested that this approach was inhumane. This was an unusual viewpoint at the time. What was being practised was considered the kindest way to help people die – ignorance as terminal bliss.

Kübler-Ross described how some patients even guessed that they were dying and wanted to talk to their loved ones, and yet were silenced by nurses and doctors obsessed with keeping them 'comfortable'. If their loved ones had been made aware of the truth, Kübler-Ross argued, there would have been the opportunity for important conversations to take place and support could have been offered. A strange and numbing politeness was controlling the hospitals; an urge to keep things neat and tidy was dictating the care dying people received. A patient might rage at their death, Kübler-Ross wrote, but it wouldn't harm them to feel this rage if they were supported through it: they could have their worries answered honestly; they could say the things they needed to say to their loved ones before they died; they could speak to their carers, and if the staff didn't have the answers, that was okay. Simply sitting with patients and showing them respect, informing them that they were dying, would lead to peace and acceptance. Knowledge didn't cause distress. The more informed patients were, the calmer they felt about what was happening to them.

Once the patient had been told the truth, Kübler-Ross argued, medical professionals needed to allow them to process the news. Patients could accept their fate if they were allowed to do so, slowly, in stages.

Fair Play Kübs — so far, all incredibly rational and reasonable.

Kübler-Ross recorded the five stages she believed patients needed to move through after diagnosis to enable them to reach an understanding that they were about to die. First up, Denial (and Isolation) — the patient doesn't believe the diagnosis: it can't be right, they need another test, they'll get better; there's a miracle cure they just need to find. Next, comes Anger — they are angry with the cancer/ malignancy: why me? I am a good person; I don't deserve to die, this isn't fair. This is followed by a little Bargaining — maybe if I pray, I will be cured? Maybe if I'm nice, God will heal me? Then: Depression – I don't want to die. This is awful, all I feel is sadness. Then on to the final stage: Acceptance — I am going to die, I am dying; I understand this. Once this stage was reached, Kübler-Ross observed, a calm fell over the patient. They might send family members away. They might withdraw because they were ready. Often when a patient was allowed enough time and space to get to the final stage, said Kübler-Ross, they died a few hours or days afterwards. The fight was over; they could see their body in its truth, in its dying state, their time here done. They had been guided through the process and now, conversations had, doubts aired, apologies made, they could die with peace and dignity. The five stages of death in a terminal illness: Denial, Anger, Bargaining, Depression, Acceptance. Or Gary, Robbie, Howard, Jason and Mark, if you will.

This all sounds great. If you have to die, make it peaceful. Have time to say your goodbyes. Know what it is you're dying from. Not sure why you've got such a beef with Kübler-Ross, Cariad ... I can imagine that if I was dying of a terminal illness, those might be the stages I'd go through ... WAIT A GRIEVING MINUTE – WHAT DOES THIS HAVE TO DO WITH GRIEF?

Yeah, exactly my bloody thought. This theory has nothing to do with grieving. It is about <u>the dying</u>.

> MIC DROP
> *Moonwalks into coffin*
> *Jumps out again because I'm scared*

Yes, Kübler-Ross's Five Stages model was written for people who were dying (of a terminal illness) – not those left behind. This was not written for you.

THIS. WAS. NOT. WRITTEN. FOR. YOU.

The majority of patients described in her book are dying of cancer. Not an unpopular choice of death, even today, but certainly not how all people die. *On Death and Dying* is an excellent manual for those supporting the terminally ill. In fact, do you know what the subtitle is? No, because no one bloody brings that up when they're giving you 'helpful' advice about moving through the Five Stages and getting over grief. Are you ready? *On Death and Dying: What the Dying Have to Teach Doctors, Nurses, Clergy and Their Own Families*. I KNOW. Nothing to do with grieving. You might as well pick up a book called *On Cars and Driving: What Cars Have to Teach Drivers, Passengers, Clergy and Their Owners* and then read bits out to someone who's grieving, insisting that it's relevant to them. 'Honestly, I'm just trying to help you, did you put the clutch down smoothly? That can really affect your braking and why haven't you accepted they're dead yet? Oh, you're crying again! Come on, we've been through this: mirror, signal, acceptance!'

The Five Stages make sense as a theory when you realise Kübler-Ross was originally directing it at patients who were dying. There is a clear ending here – death – which is not the case with grieving. There is no clear end to grief. It's infuriating that the context of Kübler-Ross's original book has been forgotten and we've been left with the myth of the Five Stages. It isn't a guide for grief. It's a guide for the dying. This joyful idea that the stages can be completed, that there is an end point, encourages us (and those around us) to see our continued grief as a failure.

Academics have outed the misinterpretation of Kübler-Ross's theory and point to decades of research showing that 'most people do not grieve in stages'. Kübler-Ross herself even stated that her theory had been misunderstood. And yet, here we still are. Me, a teenager in 1998, and the young person I met at a grief event with all the access the internet has to offer in 2019 – both looking for answers at different times and finding the same ones twenty years apart. Why has the Five Stages remained so seductive?

Puts on my grief detective hat
(Sherlock Holmes-style but with coffins for earflaps and a black veil at the front.)

The potency of the Five Stages is its simplicity. It provides us with a straightforward story with which to navigate grief. It isn't chaotic or confusing: it's a straight line, a linear narrative, a beautiful beginning, middle and end. What could be more appealing during grief, the ultimate disrupter, than a calm port awaiting you after rough seas? After a death, everything in your world is turned upside down. Your emotions and heart and sleep and thoughts are the most disorganised they will ever be (the only time I've felt as confused, exhausted and emotional was after I had my first child). The most soothing thing you can tell someone in the midst of such hell is that it will get better, and it will get easier, and that it will eventually end.

My experience of grief is that it has got easier, and it has got better, but not in a linear way. It has gone backwards and forwards and sideways and knocked me over more times than I can remember. What has helped is allowing my life to grow around it. It's unsettling to say this more truthful narrative – that there is no end to the process but somehow you will learn to live with it – especially to those not in the club, or those who have just joined and are desperately looking for the exit.

And so, the Five Stages lives on, promising 'The End', promising a land where you are fine, you are happy – dammit, you are peachy – a technicolour lie that we swallow because it looks so tasty. The idea of an end to the grief process is so appealing to us that Kübler-Ross's theory has been warped, digested and assimilated into the cultural mainstream. I can't count how many times non-club members have brought it up with me as proof that they know about grief too. It fits neatly into the story structures we are most familiar with, films and television shows, which also work on linear narratives. There has to be 'The End' so the audience can leave satisfied; the story is finished, the people are changed, the lesson was learnt – that's how stories work. The Five Stages model dovetails neatly into that yearning need we have for structure. In the Hollywood version we are shown that death is sad, but then you move on and are okay. We lap up the scenes on screen that depict grief as a simple process of 'people cry, scream, wail, weep, and then find acceptance'. And after watching this hopeful narrative, we continue to look for the same simplicity in our own complicated lives.[6]

Despite our wish to bend our lives into a straight narrative, real humans aren't as straightforward as characters in a script. When someone dies, when someone is ripped from your world – whether you knew it was coming or you got a sudden phone call in the middle of the night – how you

---

[6] Incidentally, the 1993 film *Groundhog Day* directly mirrors the Five Stages process while seemingly avoiding having a death in its narrative. Bill Murray's character, Phil Connors, is trapped in time, reliving the same day over and over again until he gets it 'right'. As he struggles to accept his fate, he goes through distinct phases/days: firstly, denial of the repetitive predicament; then on to anger (he punches Ned); bargaining; depression; then acceptance. Director Harold Ramis stated that the film's writer, Danny Rubin, took Kübler-Ross's Five Stages as a model for Connors's journey. Murray works neatly through each stage until he is finished, changed for the better, happy. The result is a successful 1990s comedy. But for me it proves once again how ill-fitting the Five Stages of grief model is to human reality. It is a comfortable Hollywood version of what grief looks like.

feel about that and deal with it simply can't (and won't) be categorised into anything neat. Grief is a sprawling, screaming gaping hole of a mess that we must learn to carry. It can't be chopped up into stages and digested at will. Once we acknowledge its messiness, we can lose our shame around feeling it months or even years later.

So, we find ourselves up Grief Mountain with two cans of pop, a broken torch and a map that tells you there is no way home. What now? Without the Five Stages as our road to the village of acceptance, how do we navigate a situation that, for most of us, is the worst thing that has ever happened?

STEPHEN MANGAN
Actor and writer. Stephen's mum died when he was in his early twenties.

The idea that you can get it wrong, that you can 'do' grief wrong; the worry when you are grieving that somehow you're not normal; the idea that you might feel awful one minute and elated the next ... Your emotions are all over the place and the idea that that perhaps is because you don't care enough ... 'I should just be sad for three years; I should go around crying because my parent has died.' We don't process grief like that, that's not how it goes, especially when you're younger, I think. Those emotions come through you and then they go and then they come back and it's a sort of lifetime process.

Despite the monolith shadow of the Five Stages, it is reassuring to see that the accepted landscape of what grief should look like is rapidly changing. Other theories do exist, theories that don't squeeze grief into a neat line (you certainly won't see them used as a narrative device in a film). They are subtler, more complex, truer to the lived experience. There are many schools of thought out there to help you understand what grief is, how it works and how it will affect you. Many of them offer a softer approach to grief, a winding path to holding space for your sadness and the slow process of allowing your life to build around it. (If you want more specific information, I have listed some resources and books at the end of this one.)

Let me help you dip your toes into grief academia and tell you about one theory I came across that blew my mind. This theory revolutionised how I viewed my grief. Reading it was the first time I felt that someone else understood it the way I did. Developed by two academics, Margaret Stroebe and Henk Schut, it is more complicated than the Five Stages and, for me, a far better description of what real grief feels like.

Stroebe and Schut argue for a new way of tackling grief, which includes the idea of 'secondary losses' (such as the loss of a marriage after the death of a child, the loss of a home after the death of a parent, etc.).[7] Their Dual Process model posits that there should be no rush to return to a positive state of mind. (The relief I felt when I read that, to allow a griefster to be sad for however long is needed, is okay.[8])

---

[7] It's a complicated text, so this is a simplified version. I would recommend reading the original if you feel it speaks to you.

[8] There is another term known as 'complicated grief', where the grief may be extended for a very long time due to complications in the relationship or death, and which can be dealt with in a different way. I discuss this in Chapter 4.

Our internal emotional landscape is far more complex than good emotions (happiness/joy/love, etc.) and bad emotions (sadness/anger, etc.). So, just because we perceive some of our emotions as being negative (feeling sad, say), it is important to feel them because we might actually *be* sad.

Much of what I had read prior to encountering the Dual Process model was about an escape from sadness, how to move through it, which of course when you are grieving is what you want to do. It has taken me many years of my grief to understand that you can't outrun the sadness, that grief just waits. Not malevolently, but it waits until you are ready to be sad. Grief demands and deserves sadness. Our fear at feeling negative feelings can, ironically, stall us from moving through them to a place where we can carry them without breaking down.

KAYLEIGH LLEWELLYN
Writer and actor. Kayleigh lost six members of her family in one year, including her father, her young nephew, her grandfather and her grandmother, who raised her.

It's not nice to feel sad, it's not nice to cry, it's not nice falling down that rabbit hole. You feel awful for an hour and so I'm the kind of person who says, 'Let's pull ourselves up by our bootstraps, let's go for a run, let's do something ...' It's important to hold both, I think. Allow yourself to let those emotions and those chemicals out of your body.

PHILIPPA PERRY
Psychologist and author.

The thing about tears is that once you allow yourself to have them, they're not as bad as you fear they might be. They don't completely overwhelm me, or at least not much longer than an hour. Your body does get fed up with anger or tears after a while, and it's probably better to feel it and know you can handle it than it is to stick it in a box.

Dual Process acknowledges that when we are in grief, two things are happening to us at the same time, and that this is complicated and sometimes confusing. We are in the sadness/griefy/horrible bit where we cry, snot tears all over our face, wail, ache and sob. And then there is a bit where we're not crying, the breaks between the waves of pain. In these periods we may try to do the (restoration-orientated) things that make us feel better: talk, eat chocolate, watch crap telly, stare at social media, hide under the duvet, etc.[9] I experienced this as a teenager, and later on too. Most griefsters I know have admitted to long periods of feeling like they were ignoring the grief and distracting themselves. I have spoken to many *Griefcast* listeners who have opened with, 'Oh, I feel so bad. I know I should be thinking about it more but instead I'm ...'

---

[9] There is a distinction between restoration-orientated activities – where you are resting from grief – and deep-denial activities, such as getting wasted, taking drugs, doom-scrolling ... which are not restoration activities.

I felt like this. Especially at the start. I felt guilty to not be wailing all the time. Was I disrespecting my dad by wanting a break from the crying some days? Was I doing grief wrong? Dual Process argues that 'ignoring' our grief and not feeling sad is part of the whole; we oscillate between the grief and the bits where we have a break from it. Dual Process argues that you *need* to do both in order to allow yourself time to process what's happened. You can't spend your whole day in active grief; you run out of tears, your throat hurts, eventually you'll need to go to the loo. It's helpful to take 'time off' from the grieving. Grief is hard, you need breaks from the deep sadness so that you can cope with being alive.

YASMINE AKRAM
Actress and writer. Yasmine spoke to me about the death of her Aunt Bernadette, who she was very close to growing up.

I'd never felt pain like that in my life … I kind of got to a point where I was sick of waking up in the morning and crying. 'Can I just have ten minutes where I'm not going to be covered in tears?'

REVEREND RICHARD COLES
Vicar, broadcaster and writer. Richard's husband, David, died in 2019.

I've found with grief that there are at least two levels: there's a kind of top level which means you burst into tears because you can't pick what parmesan you're going to have in the Co-op; and then there's the tectonic level where you know that deep, deep profound geological shifts are happening that you can do nothing about except just ride them, if you can.

When I first discovered the Dual Process model I breathed out and realised that I wasn't the only one who couldn't follow the path of Five Stages. Guilt that had lived with me since I was a teenager dissipated. I hadn't got it wrong.

In the year after my dad died, I began to obsessively watch soap operas. Sounds fairly harmless – but I wasn't watching, I was disappearing. When the shows were on, my brain was empty of thoughts, blissfully quiet, no pain, no grief, just a wind tunnel of neutral feelings. When I was watching television, I could throw my whole head into someone else's world. The TV schedule in those days meant you could lose hours to soaps and not even have to move from the sofa. I started with *Neighbours* at 5.35 p.m., *Home and Away* 6.00 p.m., a break for *The Simpsons*, then on to the home stretch of *Emmerdale*, *EastEnders* and *Coronation Street*. I'd found I had a gap before *EastEnders*, so that's when I added in *Emmerdale*, a show I'd never watched before, to make sure there was no quiet time for thinking. Beautiful peaceful hours of not thinking about his death.

This was 1998, before social media – a place which I imagine a lot of grievers go to nowadays so they can stop thinking about their own pain for an evening or two. I wish I'd known about Dual Process then. I wish I'd had its kind voice in my head telling me: 'This is okay, this is a necessary break from the wailing,' instead of the shame I felt for hiding. Eventually my mum stepped in. She popped her head round the living-room door, saw *Emmerdale* on the telly and said,

'Blimey Cariad, *Emmerdale*? You must be feeling shit,' and then went back to cook tea. No offence to *Emmerdale* – it's a well-made and thoughtful soap opera that lots of people love – but she was right. Three solid hours of other people's narratives was a bit much, even for me.

After my mum's quip, I began to wean myself off soaps. I started taking a break from the telly and started thinking what the hell I was going to do with my life. I slowly crawled out of the first raw year of grief. But I felt bad about the telly binging – felt that I had done something wrong, been selfish in blocking out my grief for him.

These days I can forgive myself for having needed it. It is okay to grieve in fits and starts. It is okay to forget your grief, to hide somewhere less painful and come back to it when you're ready. It's okay to find grief wiggly and repetitive – it isn't a straight line. It's okay if you are still wandering in circles or allowing Netflix to load up another episode of a show you don't care about. You're doing your best and that's okay.

Grief is both universal and unique. I can know how your heart aches but not how it aches for that person. How you cope with your grief, or work through it, or survive it, will be entirely your own experience. We do need maps for grief, but they need to be true to life (slightly ripped, tea-mug-stained with crumpled edges) to be useful. Find what works for you. Accept that this will change as you get older and other aspects of your grief come to the fore. If the Five Stages has helped you in any way, I am genuinely glad. Anything that can lead you through the mire of grief is worthwhile and to be celebrated. But for those who felt as frustrated as I did by its rules and regulations, know that there are other ways to understand the strange process of grieving. You are never doing it wrong.

Funeral Day

I wear a top from Bay Trading – brown, a muted colour, but not black; a silky black cardigan, and black, ribbed jersey, bootleg trousers. I wear the gold necklace he gave me in Turkey (which I realise I've since lost along the way). I wear the massive 'fuck-off' boots I used to stomp around in. They look like Spice Girl boots, but more goth and more Camden. Everyone at school teases me about them, but I like them because they're different and that's how I feel now: different. I plan what to wear that day like it's a night out and I feel strange about it; it's an occasion, a horrifically awful one, but still, it requires an armour.

All Hallows by the Tower (literally by the Tower of London) is the venue. There's been a church on this site since AD 675. It's the oldest church in the City of London. Across the road is a patch of land where they used to hang, draw and quarter traitors in centuries past. William Penn, who went on to found Pennsylvania, was baptised here. John Quincy Adams, sixth president of the United States, was married here. My dad, a management consultant, is having his funeral here – a City church for a man with as much of a Welsh accent as a north London boy can have.

The church itself is simple – clear glass, polished floors – just as you'd expect a church that survived the English Reformation to look, but it feels grander when you're inside, as if it's aware of its own history. We used to come here on Sundays, until my mum got fed up with the long drive and lack of mates and started taking us to the local church instead. Once I was in the land of suburban sermons and had something to compare it to, I realised just how high the quality of the All Hallows sermoning was. Having been exposed to the liturgical equivalent of a West End show every Sunday, I was now being forced to sit through parochial am-dram.

If I sound snobby, I was. I had been spoiled. The vicar at All Hallows had officiated at Judy Garland's funeral; he'd worked in Hollywood before being called upon; he knew how to reach the back of the room and make you feel as though God was genuinely communicating through him. I was on board. Our local church was sweet, like milky tea, but All Hallows was pure caffeine; they chucked out real Cadbury Creme Eggs for the congregation to catch at Easter, *and* had a real donkey coming up the aisle at Christmas. It didn't matter what your faith was, or how deeply you believed, you had a great time. I loved this church. I loved its version of Christianity – a glorious show with audience interaction, chocolate and gags thrown in.

My grandpa, Herbert (Bertie to everyone) helped fundraise to have a new disabled toilet installed in the church foyer and used to proudly take people in there to look at it. He'd lead them in with a twinkle in his eye, 'Let me show you what I've been working on … ' He couldn't hide his absolute glee that the great and good of the City of London were having to coo and aah over a new loo.

After a service, people would chat and gather. It was like a party some weeks – my dad networking, my grandpa forgetting he didn't need to any more. I'd run around, swishing past the soft Laura Ashley skirts and trying to take another biscuit before being handed another Creme Egg. It might sound like I'm making it up, but it's all true.

On this day in 1998, the funeral day, the church is packed. People are squeezed into the pews, standing at the sides, still in shock, still in disbelief. We sit at the front. I don't look behind me, just stare at my church, our church, our fun, theatrical church-world now full of funeral and loss and sadness. His running shoes are on the coffin. 'A nice touch,' everyone says. A woman my parents know sings a song. His friend, who used to be an actor, does a speech. He holds up the newspaper for that day or his death day – I don't quite remember – but it had something about space or the moon on it and everyone agreed it was apt. 'He would have loved that,' they said.

'Shoot for the moon. Dream big, kid.' Did he say that? Even then, so soon after, things had begun to blur.

I look down at my trousers, study each line of the stretchy black material. I wear them to work a year later when I get a Saturday job at the local bakery (free pastries after 6 p.m., I don't know if I've bettered it), and I wear the muted brown top and silky cardigan ensemble on holiday in Spain. One evening a boy says, 'I like your top,' and I reply, 'Thanks. I wore it at my dad's funeral.' I could never lie, even when it would have been easier and a lot less weird to have done so.

At the church, Frank Zappa's 'Peaches en Regalia', an instrumental piece my dad loved, plays as everyone leaves. It's so loud, blaring out of the speakers, it seems a bit incongruous – the church ancient and solid against this free and wild music. But it fits him and the two vying sides of his upbringing.

51

My friends are here, my brother's too. We all gather at the back of the church after the service. It feels like a party, no one quite ready to leave, too many hellos to say. I hang back and listen because I'm afraid to be wrong or say something silly to the grown-ups. Some relative I've never met before is talking to me. He just seems like an old man. He's sad my dad is dead. Yeah, me too. Me too.

Because there are so many of us in the funeral party, we have hired a coach. It's been allowed to park next to the church. That impresses me and I have a strange sensation of excitement as we get on board. It's odd, I push it away, another 'wrong' feeling. We'd never been allowed to park there – Dad always struggled to get a parking spot – and yet here we are – an odd, banal privilege of being dead: great parking.

As the coach reverses away from the church out onto the road, I look down again at my trousers, the ribbed material, the lines going up and down. That way I don't have to see the coffin going into the hearse. Hearse. Everyone keeps using that word. 'We're not in the funeral car, it's too much,' Mum says.

If you'd asked me what we did next, for many years I couldn't have told you. The day ended there, a blank until later, when there's a pub and egg sandwiches, more relatives. A lady in leopard print (unusual for my family) wearing a huge hat and lipstick – she's laughing, and my grandpa is talking to her. A tiny shred of his formidable charm and patter still left in him, but nothing like he was … nothing at all. She's a cousin, a second or third one. That's mostly what I hear at the pub, 'Oh, they're a cousin.' I eat too much cake because no one stops me.

Years later, I want to fill in the blanks. Someone asks me about his cremation, and I realise exactly what it is I have removed. I can't remember it. How strange to not even know you don't have a memory until you reach into the drawer to look for it and it's not there. I know he was cremated. Where did we go in the coach, before the pub? There is no memory ... just a blank. I stare at the empty drawer in my filing cabinet memory: 'What happened, please?'

I wait.

'You sure?' the drawer seems to ask me.

'Yes, I'm sure.'

'Okay,' says the drawer, like it had just been waiting to be asked.

And then there it is, the reality of the cremation – terrible, painful. I had deleted it for a reason. I didn't want this bit of the day to live. All the hubbub gone, just the family and a few friends, a north London crematorium (the one everyone uses): pale pews, new wood, very clean. No grandeur to distract you from the truth. Far too real. That was the worst part. When he went, when the coffin ... the curtain, when it felt like they took him. Like it was finally done. A rip, a raw cut of my soul. Just grief now. Just us now, on the other side of the curtain – a terrible play with no laughter in it.

It shocked me – what you can still forget, the things your eyes pass over. Oh yes, *there*'s the day. The end? The goodbye? No, it's not there, it ends in a buffet and some people chatting. It doesn't end with him leaving. He didn't leave. He's just not here, he's away. He died when I was fifteen, he's not dead yet.

53

Wave — 1998

Summer

So much is blurred. Sunburn on a shoulder from years ago. The days, weeks, months after he died are rubbed in together. I can barely remember the week of the immediate aftermath. When did I start sleeping in Mum's bed? When did I go back to school? When did I take the exams I didn't care about any more?

Grief is often described as coming in waves. A fitting way to describe something you have no control over. Grievers stand like King Canute on the shoreline. They bark at the waves, scream at them, tell them they rule this shore, but the waves don't listen. Some waves are worse than others, some roar.

Autumn

I remember coming home, teatime, on my own in the house. Being alone allowed the weeping. I wouldn't do this in front of others. No one is to know how bad I feel. Too risky. Not safe, keep it together Lloyd. Keep it together till you get home. Roll your eyes, roll your skirt up. You don't care, you don't care. They think you don't care. Now, alone, home from school, I weep and cry and sob and weep. There is no embarrassment here in being this snotty, howling wolf-child, wailing like a Trojan wife.

That's how grief felt at fifteen – a mess, too much. It's all I could breathe now, grief. There was no room for me, who I was, who I was going to be. I was just grief, grief was me.

I wailed, no one could hear me. I sat on the sofa and shouted to the ceiling, to the corner above the bookshelf, in fact – in case, like a ghost, he was hovering there, a middle-aged Dead Dad Casper. 'Where the fuck are you?' I shouted.

Stop it. Stop it Cariad. Stop this mess. It's too much, this is too much.

I pulled myself together, dragged myself down the hallway to the kitchen, clutching my tea tray with the sweet woodland scene on it – hedgehogs foraging, blackberries – hands shaking. So much anger. My hands itched. I took the glass and the plate, with its sandwich crumbs, off the tray. Damage but not too much damage. Not unanswerable damage. Squeezing the stupid white tray, knuckles white, I threw it to the floor. It smashed. A large chunk snapped off in a diagonal slash. Just one large chunk. I felt better for a breath and then, no, this was more embarrassing, mortifying. I was mortified at my lack of control. Now a tray was broken, now someone might know I was sad. That was slippy. If they knew I was sad, I might have to talk. I didn't want to talk. I didn't want to talk about something that hadn't really happened. He hadn't died, he can't have, because it doesn't make sense. So he must just be away.

But you saw him Cariad, you saw him …

'Where the fuck are you? Are you here?'

I tidied up, made the kitchen a calm place of no emotions. Smooth, quiet, controlled. All good. Later, I tell my mum the tray fell off the side. She gives me a look.

Numb now, bruised and numb. The howling gives way to a peace. It's a release, but it feels like it will never end when it's happening. The waves recede for a brief while, time enough to brace yourself, to form rocks in your heart so that you can take the crash and roar of pain next time. No idea when, or where. Try and save it up for when you get home. Dig your nails into your palms, like you do in maths exams to save yourself from crying and admitting you don't know the answers.

'Where the fuck are you?'

Winter

A trip to New Zealand to avoid Christmas, to see relatives on your side who we've never met. The descendants of my Great-Aunt Phyllis, my dad's aunt – Lloyds on the other side of the world. It's a trip, a holiday! It's like it always was: we travel and see things. You're not there, but perhaps you're on a call, at a meeting, arriving later. It doesn't feel so wrong. It feels absent, not dead.

They are so kind, so thoughtful, we are so far away. I meet my Great-Aunt Anne – my grandpa's sister. She is funny and bright and tells me of Great-Aunt Kitty, the first woman in Bridgend to wear trousers. I beam inside from talking to her, from feeling at home. To feel at home with my family. Loud, fiery me. I fit. Somewhere I fit. I'm not just like you; there are women like me, too – Lloyds. Why didn't I know this? Why is this new information?

It's just days before Christmas. We're staying in a summerhouse, a 'batch' they call it. There's pavlova the size of your head, and I don't quite understand why, but we watch *Xena: Warrior Princess* singing carols in the

57

sunshine. My brother and I are confused but we laugh a lot, eat barbequed food and go bungee-jumping and it's a holiday.

There's a phone call. I'm standing in the living room and then I'm not – I'm in the bedroom, climbing up to the top bunk. I don't know how I got here. I don't remember going into the bedroom. Grandpa is dead. Bertie, Herbert, his dad. He's died. Now, I'm weeping uncontrollably, in front of everyone as I try to get up on the bunkbed. I don't care. I don't care. Because now he's gone. He who could talk, the charmer, the orator, the POW survivor, the Bridge over the River Kwai builder, the solicitor, the flirt, the fierce holder-together of all of us – he who was your dad and who was so much to me. Another rock in my life tumbled away.

I cry so much, the whole house does, we're all related to him somehow. Everyone is weeping. It's Christmas in a few days and my brother forgets and sleeps in. He doesn't believe us when he finally wakes in the afternoon, and we tell him. We have to turn the telly on to prove it's Christmas Day. So strange this world is now. You gone, him gone. What's the fucking point? I stop looking for you. I don't know where you are, I realise. Nothing makes any sense.

Years later, I read that you have to go through each season without them. You have to see the leaves fall, the cold and grey arrive, the new flowers appear and then feel the sun, without them. Each season your brain tells you, 'They didn't see this, they didn't smell this, or feel this warmth. They are gone.'

They are gone.

2

Great Expectations

How Should Grief Behave?

So now we understand that grief isn't a linear process, that it goes up, then down, and then whizzes back to the beginning again like a badly played pinball game, I want to go deeper into our cultural history of grief. What did ideas about grief look like before the reign of the Five Stages? What else has shaped our expectations of how we grieve?

Let me introduce you to Gwendolyn Lightcraving. Here she is, standing wistfully in the doorway of her smart townhouse, thick fog looming in the lamplight of the street. In the mist, Gwendolyn descends the front steps, her black lace gloves avoiding the already damp iron railings. On the cobbled pavement she steps over a puddle, the grey clouds of the dull sky reflected in it. Light drizzle begins to fall as she climbs into her horse-drawn carriage. She pulls down her black veil, covering her face, dries her eyes on a black lace handkerchief, lifts her large, black skirt and, gathering the many heavy layers of fabric, swishes inside. She taps the roof, and a grim-faced, top-hatted coachman pulls the reins tight, and they clip-clop off down the cobbled street.

Thank you. Students, please answer the following question after reading the above text. You have five minutes to finish the exam. Is Gwendolyn:

    A) a butcher?
    B) a Jedi?
    C) A VICTORIAN WIDOW?

The answer is … C! Yes! Congratulations, five shilling-points and a side order of Huzzah! You recognised that Gwennie was a Victorian widow, probably off to her husband's funeral, a man who no doubt died of cholera while visiting a factory he owned and breathing near some infected boot-polish air. (Gwennie will now find out he was up to his eyes in debt from gambling; she'll be unable to pay the debtors, so will have to head off to the workhouse to pay for his immoral behaviour. Don't blame me, blame Gordon Lightcraving – he was a scoundrel.)

Much has been written about the devastation left by the twentieth century's two world wars. Most of us are familiar with the stiff-upper-lip, keep-calm-and-carry-on attitude to death that was said to have accompanied them. But before that? Before that was an age which set the tone for stoicism. The Victorians.

Grief and mourning today is still fundamentally shaped by Queen Vic and her big black dress. The original widow, Queen Victoria remained in full mourning clothes after the loss of her husband, Prince Albert, until her own death forty years later. Her attitude to grief and the role that Victorian society played in controlling and regulating this emotional state is still often accepted as 'normal' for grieving today, rather than an attitude we have inherited. From funerals to etiquette, to the time we're allowed to remain sad, so much of our grief vocabulary comes from the nineteenth century. The formality and societal expectations around grief were set in the age of colonialism, capitalism and jellied puddings. Now, as we begin to analyse and deconstruct the many legacies of this

61

era, let us also investigate how some of our death and grief traditions are hand-me-downs that no longer fit.

Unlike the Five Stages, which policed our private processes, the Victorians were interested in directing the public process of grief. If you have ever felt ashamed of your grief for its messiness, doubted if your emotional responses were 'correct' after a death, or experienced being told to snap back to happiness after a certain period of time, you'll find the roots of these judgements buried in the 1800s. Grieving today is haunted by these shadows. They are a hangover as loud as our strange desire to drag pine trees indoors in December and cover them in tinsel and tangled lights.[1] There is still a Victorian whiff of bergamot and roses around our grieving that's impossible to shake.

Unlike the Five Stages, which searched for a bow to tie the strands of grief together, the Victorians sought to control grief with rules and regulations. They didn't care what stage you were going through, as long as you finished it within the allotted time. And these are rules we're committed too still. Most of us have attended a quiet, sombre, badly sung, hymn-filled, black-clothes-wearing funeral that any Victorian industrialist would have been proud of. When we've been to a funeral that defies these norms – one where colourful clothes are requested, where pop music is played and jokes are made in the eulogy – we feel the frisson of tradition being broken. The quiet, respectful mourner, the

---

[1] Yes, I'm sorry, the Victorians also did the PR for Christmas. You need to thank Germany and paganism for your living-room winter festival.

black clothes, even a horse-drawn funeral carriage,[2] are still recognisable markers in our modern life. And just as we know what a funeral should look like, there is a way we expect grief to behave, a timeline we expect mourning to follow, that is directly linked to the Victorians' timeline of 'polite grief'. As many of us in the club will tell you, we've often felt the lingering silent pressure to have moved on, be cheery, not be sad about the death after a 'decent' amount of time has been allotted to us by society.

The Victorians did not live in a vacuum, they reacted to what had come before them. Many of their death and grief rules and regulations were because of the chaos of earlier decades (from graverobbers to graveyards literally overflowing, but more on the fun Georgians later). Now, with a little acknowledgement of our debt to them, we can sweep away many of their more rigid ideas. As we learn to accept our own wiggly grief path (does it help if you imagine a sort of Charlie Brown-style dust bowl squiggle?), we see that this mess of feelings we are experiencing is normal. It is not a timed process, but a lived one. And yet those who haven't lived it will still have ideas about how we *should* be feeling, based on many antiquated ideas about how grieving people should act. (NB, we don't all behave like Queen Vic and that's okay.) The outside world may look at us a little strangely, 'Still grieving? After a *whole year*? Is everything ... okay?'[3], or at the opposite end of the scale, 'Not crying every day? Well then, so glad you're over it finally.'

---

[2] I've already seen two horse-drawn funerals, just this year, and I don't live in East London, or the past.

[3] Yes, just my dad is STILL dead, so I STILL feel sad. Weird, I know.

We know we don't need to search for an ending for our grief, so let us also free ourselves from the stigma of behaving 'inappropriately' too, leaving us with a truth, a mess that is entirely our own. Then we can have the freedom of admitting that a civilised demeanour for an uncontrollable set of emotions is simply impossible to live up to and doomed to fail. Why are we so afraid to let grief be the mess that we know it is?

The Victorians were into death. They liked it as much as we like fifteen-second videos of grandparents learning hip-hop routines. Of course, death was present in their world in a way that is hard to conceive of today. For them, life expectancy was low, child mortality high, diseases were rife, and the power of good hygiene was only just being discovered. In contrast, we have achieved a distance through medicalisation, protecting us from death's most ugly traits, that they could only have dreamt of. The deaths they experienced were often at home – real, tragic and visceral. Death was terrifyingly uncontrollable.

As with so many elements of Victorian society, from sewers to education to science, there was a push to create order out of chaos, to engineer their way to calm. This calm began with burials. Bodies needed to be buried properly, in a way that they hadn't been previously, for reasons of decorum and to control disease. The Victorians began to regulate not just death but the rituals around death. Maybe grief could be contained as well as the bodies? Why not chuck in some regulations too about the required thickness of mourning cards, and how long a widow should be sad for?

The cultural picture of a proper funeral – a dignified widow, a respectful service, the images we turn to still – isn't how grief has always been. We didn't always expect the grieving to be quiet and respectful. The process of burial and grief mattered to the Victorians, not just out of respect for the dead, but from a moral standpoint. They couldn't separate the dead from the ceremony surrounding them, the emotional from the material. It's easy for us to have inherited these expectations and not understand what caused them to be so important or fixed.

Prior to the mass late nineteenth-century tidy-up, the decades before Queen Vic and her lovely big black dress, were a time of death chaos. It can feel as though the Victorian era obliterated many of the grief traditions that came before it, but the reason we have such a slippery grasp of how we mourned and grieved prior to this time is because death was a less regulated process then. For Georgians, the pomp and ceremony of it all was important, but it wasn't controlled and nationalised into a uniform. They were more interested in getting people buried, and fast: people were dying (a lot) and often from contagious diseases. The job of the burial was to get rid of a body with respect and contain the spread of whatever they had died from. Most ordinary people would simply be wrapped in shrouds and carried by male relatives to the churchyard (women were often encouraged to take part at a distance, so the ceremony wouldn't be ruined by their crying or fainting).[4]

---

[4] Ah, the pleasing reliable longevity of the patriarchy.

In 1831, just six years before Victoria's reign began, there was a cholera epidemic in Britain which would kill over 52,000 people. This, combined with a burgeoning population, meant that the graveyards were filling up rapidly. Hoping to solve the 'too many dead bodies' problem, a decision was made to start shoving multiple adults into the same hole and not cover them properly, in what one might call 'a health and safety nightmare'. So, to deal with the 'bodies piling up' problem, the authorities opted to build more churches and more graveyards. This worked in the countryside, but in urban areas, where there was a lack of space, the dead continued to be stacked on top of each other. Instead of going deeper into the earth, it was easier just to raise the ground. Some churches even had the ground level brought up to the windows to accommodate all the dead (suddenly all those horror films featuring the dead rising from their graves start to make sense, because at one point you could be singing 'All Things Bright and Beautiful' and then glance through the stained glass to see Uncle Harry's very dead head popping up through the topsoil).

Of course, if you were a Victorian you would want to regulate this. It was a mess. Grieving is bad enough without dead bodies popping up in graveyards like an overstuffed snack cupboard pouring out crisps. To counteract this chaos, grand new urban graveyards were built away from churches. These were well-ordered spaces, designed to be pleasant and peaceful places to visit, where the dead could rest with dignity. If you've ever wandered around Kensal Green, Norwood, Abney Park, Highgate or Brompton Park cemeteries in London, St James's in Liverpool or the

Necropolis in Glasgow, you can imagine how calm and serene these great designs must have once felt. If it worked there, then surely people could be just as well ordered?

The Victorians regulated, legislated, tidied and reformed wherever they could. What would it have been like for Gwendolyn, the Victorian widow?[5] Prep your widow's weeds, your black lace, veils, sashes, horses, mourning cards, mourning coats, mourning caps, mourning wax, mourning wreaths, mourning jellies (YES, JELLIES), armbands, cloaks, coffins, candles, and bow your head in beatific sorrow, as we enter *Deep Mourning*.[6] Gwendolyn couldn't have just worn black and hoped for the best.[7] She would have had to buy a completely new black outfit every time (one for each death she experienced – probably a fair few in her lifetime).[8] Crepe was the fabric required as it didn't combine well with other clothing,[9] which meant Gwennie now owned a special grief dress that couldn't be paired with anything else in her wardrobe. Jewellery had to be made of jet, a black stone which isn't too jolly-looking – or if Gwennie had felt fancy she could have opted for the deceased's hair to be woven into a brooch or necklace.[10] Men were also expected to wear a brand-new

[5] Grieving by day, fighting street crime by night. She is *The Widow* (starring Matt Damon, in cinemas now).

[6] *Deep Mourning*, the sequel to *The Widow* (starring Matt Damon, in cinemas now).

[7] Victorians didn't invent wearing black to mourn the dead. In fact, oddly, the reason black is a traditional colour to wear is, it was thought that if veiled in black the mourner would be invisible to the dead – a protection against an unwanted visitation from a really boring dead relative, I suppose.

[8] Count yourself lucky: you could wear your smart work trousers for the church bit and get away with cleaning the tomato sauce stains off in the loos.

[9] Just like that top you've got that you never wear because it doesn't go with jeans.

[10] The nineteenth-century version of having a picture of them on the lock screen of your phone.

black suit, a tie, gloves and a hat to each funeral; dedicated etiquette guides even gave descriptions of the appropriate lengths and widths for black silk hatbands. Details, darling, details. Such was the desire and need to fulfil these rituals that mourning warehouses sprang up, like gothic Primarks. Jay's of Regent Street, London, was one of the most famous – a multitude of floors on which to purchase your grief, the proper way.

A 'decent' Victorian funeral would kick off with two 'mutes' standing outside your front door. The mutes were essentially paid mourners, dressed appropriately, who would later lead the funeral procession. They would carry crepe-covered wands and wear frock coats and top hats (strangely these were bright pink – JOKE ... they were also black). Even the door-knocker of the house was meant to be covered with crepe: black for the death of an adult, white for a younger person. Grief was public, loud, demonstrative. Everyone would be expected to know you were suffering.

Let's not forget the dead's sartorial look. Did you care about your loved one? Do you want them to have the correct bed for all eternity? Right, well then get your wallet out because you're going to need a strong coffin – made of good wood, with a white satin lining, mattress, pillow, sheets – covered with a fine black cloth; even the nails and handles should be silvered. Black ostrich feathers for the horses; silk scarves, gloves, hatbands, cloaks for the coachmen. A middle-class funeral was an extravaganza[11] which could easily cost well over £1,000, not including the tomb for the coffin.

---

[11] Serving coffins for days, now take it to the churchyard! *ghost sashays away*. (I would fully watch a ghost *RuPaul's Drag Race*, and I'm pretty sure I wouldn't be the only one.)

It's no wonder that when Charles Dickens died in 1870, he prepared his last wishes to defend against this grand ritual. His will stated that he wanted to be 'buried in an inexpensive, unostentatious, and strictly private manner; that no public announcement be made of the time or place of my burial; that at the utmost not more than three plain mourning coaches be employed; and that those who attend my funeral wear no scarf, cloak, black bow, long hat-band, or other such revolting absurdity'. Did he have his request granted? No, Tiny Tim, of course not. Dickens was buried in Poet's Corner, Westminster Abbey, against his last wishes. His grave was left open for three days to allow public viewings. He was considered too important a public figure to be quietly buried in his local cathedral, Rochester, as he had set down in his will. The Victorians understood the power of a funeral, what a death ritual could tell you about the dead person's power and status (it's a trope that very much lingers with us today).

This obsession with the correct rituals and uniforms meant that for lower-income families, expectations were always going to be impossible to meet. Burial clubs were created, where families would put aside a few pennies each week and then pool them with other poor families to ensure a proper funeral could be provided when the time came. These savings were prioritised over food or rent, because to end up with a pauper's funeral meant your soul would be left to wander for eternity, never at peace in the 100-per-cent confirmed afterlife.

Victorian rules extended to the period of time you were to wear mourning clothes, a period which varied depending on your relationship to the deceased.[12] Widows were expected to wear black for two years. Gwendolyn would not have been required to enter society for twelve months, the first stage of deep mourning lasting a year and a day from when her husband died. Only after this could she have graduated to second-stage mourning, when she could have lifted her black veils and perhaps allowed herself to wear grey or – *gasps and sniffs lace handkerchief* – purple. The second stage lasted nine months and was followed by half-mourning for a further three months. If Gwendolyn had been forced to remarry for financial reasons, she would have had to return to her mourning THE DAY AFTER the wedding. What a buzzkill for your next marriage. ('Yes, I love you too darling, but do you remember Fred, my first husband? Oh, he was lovely. I have his hair just here if you want to see, darling? Darling?!')

The Victorians also had set mourning times for anyone related to you. 'For children, if above ten years old, from six months to a year; below that age, from three to six months; for an infant six weeks and upwards.' Brothers and sisters got six to eight months; uncles and aunts, three to six; cousins, or uncles and aunts by marriage, six weeks to three months; distant friends or relations, three weeks upwards. So precise, as if grief can be measured by weeks and months. We know it can't now, we know it's preposterous to expect someone to follow such a strict code, but have we got rid of it, or just extended the terms and conditions?

We still live with an 'appropriate duration for grief' — an amorphous date from the death after which we are encouraged (by polite smiles or subject changing) to not go on about it any more. There is a point when society asks you to stop showing your upset so visibly. It is no longer plotted rigidly on a calendar, but as any griefster will tell you, it is often a surprise to non-members that you are 'still' sad after a year. You are cajoled and willed to a place where you can speak easily without messy tears ('Ah yes, so sad ... he had a good innings, he would have hated being ill for a long time etc. etc. etc.'). These are the scraps and remnants of Victorian grief. We judge grievers who refuse to contain their sadness because 150 years ago, someone[13] set down and marked how long that sadness should last, next to how long a black silk hatband should be, and the two were considered of equal importance.

REVEREND RICHARD COLES

You slightly feel that it's bad manners, don't you, not to be the perky person? ... There is a sort of impatience I think with mourning, because it's boring. Mourning is boring. Grief is boring.

KAYLEIGH LLEWELLYN

I wanted normality, I wanted a chance to laugh and to sit in the pub with my friends and there was so much

---

[13] Probably a man — sorry folks, but it's likely.

concern in my head about what people would think of me if they knew I'd been through so many deaths and saw me laughing in the pub. They'll think I'm cold; they'll think I don't care about people, they'll think I'm heartless; they'll think I'm crazy ...

We have a sense of when society feels we should move on – we certainly feel it when we've overstayed our emotional welcome. We all know inherently when tears are embarrassing, eliciting hurried apologies, instead of allowing ourselves to break without guilt. In grief we feel ashamed of our emotional outbursts over 'nothing' – and yet isn't it fine to cry in Sainsbury's because you saw their favourite yoghurt? Because it *was* their favourite, and they're dead and now you can't buy it any more without feeling silly. Isn't that human? To allow the tears to appear and roll down your cheeks just because ... you're grieving. Because someone died and is gone.

We can't choose when these moments happen to us, we can't save them for a private sphere. Can we allow ourselves to be a mess of grief when the world would like us to clean up on aisle four? If we weep and snot and wail over a small thing, let us; sometimes it can be the smallest, most mundane thing that sets us off. If it's years later and for no discernible reason that today we still feel the raw burn of our grief, that's okay. If we are laughing next to a hospital bed, or at a funeral, because of the absurdity of it all, that's not disrespect, that's shock and confusion and sometimes the plain joy of the very real things that happen next to and alongside someone dying.

The cultural picture of a proper funeral, a dignified widow, a respectful service – this isn't how grief has always been. This is still (in terms of British history) a relatively new way of expecting grief to behave. And these are the expectations that can lead to shame surrounding grief – shame that you cannot move on as quickly as others expect, that you are not as sad as you should be, that you are laughing before others think you should be able to experience joy – all views that come from seeing grief as a fixed state rather than an individual experience. What freedom could we find if we released ourselves from this idea of a fixed grief which has not evolved with us?

Grief does not behave itself. It can't be contained in stages or timed durations. We lose sight of our grief when we search for what's right, moral or expected of us. And when we lose sight of our grief, we lose sight of ourselves, what we are truly feeling, which makes it harder to understand how we can build a life around the pain.

Any griefster today could be forgiven for longing for an enforced period of mourning. It would be nice to tell the world to leave you alone for a year, no? But of course, the problem with this 'rule' is its innate ruleness. Placing any restrictions on a mourning period leaves no room for flexibility. It declares that grief should be the same for everyone. For it to be stipulated that today is the day you are allowed to smile again is, of course, absurd. Grief doesn't behave like that. If only we could promise that the first year will be hard, and that everything after that will be half better. The Victorian impulse to regulate, to time, to measure, worked well for them as engineers and industrialists, but grief doesn't behave like a bridge or a railway.

Yet there are elements of the Victorian model that we can feel some nostalgia for. They built a society that elevated grief. Grief was given special clothes, vocabulary, stationery. It was a society which understood that grief is a truly painful process that calls for space and symbolism. We have thrown away the formality that gave a purpose to those rules. We are sent flowers and, by the time the blooms have died, it's expected that our feelings will have changed too. We don't regularly wear black armbands any more;[14] other people have no idea we are grieving or suffering. We don't wrap our house in black crepe. The wider world has no idea who we have lost and how long ago it was. We have kept the Victorians' sense of judgement, but we've thrown away their grand sense of grief, the reverence and the clear signalling for grief, which could help us now.

The desire to communicate to the world that you are not okay today came up time and time again when talking to guests on my podcast. So many of us (me included) could recall a time when we'd wished people had known that we were still grieving without us having to tell them. We talked about it so much, in fact, that a very brilliant artist, Camille Bozzini, got in touch with me. She wanted to design some badges that would work like a black crepe bow on your front door, something to let the world know

---

[14] There are exceptions, of course: black armbands are still regularly worn at sporting events and military ceremonies. Their presence lingers, and I think most of us recognise their meaning without ever having worn one ourselves. But the idea of just popping one on to go to the shops after a family member has died has certainly been lost to a more formal idea of how we remember and honour someone.

you were grieving. We worked together on four designs. The first one simply stated, 'Please be kind, I'm grieving', on a round pin badge, a hand reaching out to another hand in bright pastels; the second featured a ghost with a hat on, saying 'DDC' (Dead Dad Club) at the top, and 'I'm in the Club' along the bottom. A third had a ghost with a flower on her hat, saying 'DMC (Dead Mum Club) – I'm in the Club'. Finally, there was a beautifully simple wreath of flowers, which said: 'I'm in the club'. Later, we even added a DSC (Dead Sibling Club) badge and a DPC (Dead Partner Club) badge.

The badges were designed so that those who understood their symbols would be able to reach out to the wearer and say: 'Me too, I'm sorry, I hope today is okay.' The badges sold out every time we did a run of them. I posted them out all over the world. A teacher bought thirty so that she could keep a pot at school for any pupils who needed them. A listener emailed to say she had been on a train heading to Brighton and a fellow passenger had noticed the floral-wreath badge she was wearing, and they had got talking about their losses – a grief swap occurred, purely because of the badge. We'd created an accessory to allow those who wished it, to say proudly: 'I'm grieving. I'm not ashamed, I'm not going to hide this away, this is an important part of who I am.'

At first I was surprised at how many people wanted a badge, at how many messages I received about restocking. And then I remembered how I wished I'd had one. How I wished that society had been made more aware of how thin my skin was at certain points. There are so few symbols left for us in the twenty-first century, so few grand Victorian ways to say: 'I'm feeling pretty shit over here.' I'm sure there were many nineteenth-century widows who wanted to throw off their mountains of mourning skirts, but I'm also sure there were widows who took comfort from the fact that the world expected no more of them at that moment than melancholy. As Gwendolyn lived her life wrapped in black, then maybe someone in a shop may have been more careful to catch her eye and smile, a friend may have made the effort to squeeze her hand as they parted because, they bloody knew, this was a grieving person.

Each order for a badge would come with the same story – a longing to have grief acknowledged publicly without needing to scream or shout. It struck me early on, as I read each message, as the extraordinary stories of connection came back to me, that this wasn't merch or even just a badge. It was powerful symbolism for 'the club', a physical embodiment of not being alone in it.

Our grief is what we have left of the person. It's proof of so much. Of how we loved them, how we fought with them, the hurts we gained, the love we still hold. Our grief deserves a space in our society. A space, not morbid, frightening or controlled, but a modern manifestation of what the Victorians knew: that grief takes time. So many of my guests spoke of the feeling of frustration, of fury, that people don't know how you feel, don't know that you are grieving.

SIMON THOMAS
TV presenter and writer. Simon's first wife, Gemma, died very suddenly of blood cancer in 2017.

I remember vividly walking into that fast-food restaurant, and here is everyday normal life right in front of you: the sound of kids messing around, arguing over on those ruddy iPads they've stuck in McDonald's, the sound of the chip fryer crackling, just the sights and sounds of a normal Friday night. But to me it was an absolute affront. It was an offensive affront I was feeling because I was in the most bewildering, broken, horrible, frightening place I've ever been launched into, and yet here was a normal Friday night at a McDonald's and I was so close to shouting, I came within millimetres of just going, 'What the f— is wrong with you?'

It's so easy in grief to feel isolated. In studies of the brain, it has been shown that the area that lights up when you're depressed is the area that lights up when you are in grief. Grief physiologically isolates you from everyone – the feeling that no one understands, no one gets what you're going through, is real. This is what your emotions are telling you and, in a way, they're right. No one does understand the completely unique nature of your grief. Grief is entirely unique to you and that person; your relationship with them was like no one else's, and your grief too is completely different from anyone else's.

It is easy to focus on the absurdity of the Victorian etiquette for grief, but what their rules, regulations and control did was to constantly emphasise how important the death was. We can now acknowledge how helpful it would be to allow a space in society for grief; when someone asks how you are, to be able to say without embarrassment: 'I'm grieving.' For them to understand what that means. In some ways, I feel sad that we don't have black veils, black bows on front doors, a mourning period respected by all, that honour given to grief. I want people to know, 'He's dead, he died. I'm still here, still standing, but my grief is still here, a part of my story.' I want to reach out to others when I see they are also in grief and say, 'Me too, I have walked a path so like yours and I made it through some of the worst bits. You can say their name to me, you can cry, you can be in grief – and I will stay. I will listen. I know there is a club, and I am a proud member of it.'

Let's throw away the guilt, the shame, the mourning dates and rigid rules,[15] but let us keep the importance of our deaths and our griefs. Let us share that we knew someone, that we loved someone and that they died. Today is an anniversary, today is a birthday, today is just a day I miss them. Once we allow ourselves some space to be in grief, we can lose the shame of doing it 'wrong' or 'inappropriately'; we can allow ourselves more compassion than the Victorians did – to grieve past a deadline, to grieve for as long as we need to.

Let's jump out of the carriage and take what works for us now, cherry-picking what is useful. Let us grieve loudly. Let no one say, 'It's too much, it's been too long, it's time.' If Gwennie wants to smile two days after the funeral, dye her hair blonde and move to Paris, then go for it, Gwennie. Grief shows up in our lives in extraordinary ways. The sooner we stop expecting anything of it and start listening instead to what it needs of us, the easier it will become for us to carry.

---

[15] Let's keep the mourning jellies, though – they sound quite fun.

Round and Round and Round

Comfort

Runny boiled egg. Lie on floor. Watch washing machine.

(written in a diary I bought at Miss
Selfridge, 18 October 2000)

I think it's night, it's dark outside, but it could just be winter. I'm in my mum's kitchen, or my kitchen, as it was then. She hadn't done it up yet. Hadn't knocked the wall down like she always said she wanted to. Like she finally did, years later. It stopped feeling like our house and became her house then.

She hadn't changed anything since we moved in in 1989, except the flooring. Beige lino with a white outline to indicate tiles, imitating posh brown marble and not quite succeeding. She'd bought a cheap offcut that didn't fit the room, which left a bubble of excess that eventually folded over and became cracked, a large fault line across the ground.

Mum and me aren't really eating anything at the moment (Mum and I, sorry Dad). I don't want to eat anything, it's as if my stomach is only digesting grief and sadness, and food is an extra it can't tolerate. The only thing that my palate can cope with is Heinz Cream of Tomato Soup. In the evening we share a tin of its tomatoey-red goodness and a toasted bagel cut in two. I add ham to my half and

79

my vegetarian mother adds cheese and dairy-free spread to hers (though no one is allergic to dairy in the house). 'This is bearable,' I think as I eat. I know at one point I weigh seven stone, because I stand on the scales out of curiosity and note to myself that it's not much. But I don't feel like much of a person, so that feels about right. I am not anorexic, but I recognise in myself the danger of going too close to the edge of control, enjoying the calm I feel when I don't eat, allowing my emotions to fill me up instead of food. I can feel myself creeping towards finding the answers in hunger rather than facing my pain.

It's dark outside. I am in the kitchen but there is no soup, so I boil an egg in our egg pan. (You don't really appreciate the parental egg pan till you have to move out of home and realise you need and do not have one.) My mum's is covered in a retro 1970s brown-and-yellow flower pattern. Its once-black insides are almost white from so much egg-boiling. I pour water into the pan. I boil an egg. Then I realise the washing machine is on. It's doing my favourite bit – spinning round and round. I pour cold water on the egg, peel off its fragile shell and skin, then slide myself down to the floor. I am lying on the floor, watching the washing spinning round and round, eating my egg, and it's the happiest I've been for some time.

I didn't know why then, but now I realise it's because I was not thinking. For the first time in a while, my brain had paused. The washing machine was better than a soap opera, nothing to identify with or draw me in or upset me, just a glass circle, ever-moving, swirling, spinning, cleaning things, and getting something done in the midst of all the unbearable pain.

'For God's sake, let us sit upon the ground and tell sad stories of the death of kings.'[1]

Richard II

(I'm sure he didn't do this with a boiled egg, but he might have felt better if he had.)

---

[1] William Shakespeare, *Richard II*, Act III, sc. ii.

Seventeen

I'm seventeen when I do a weekend self-help-course-thing. I come from a family quite big on self-help-course-things. My parents loved a self-help seminar. We used to go on family ones. Once, they got involved with a self-help therapy organisation dodgy enough to be branded as a cult by the *Daily Mail*. They liked to talk, work things through, chew them over with people trained in LA. I have been raised to talk, to analyse, to hold myself accountable, even in grief. I have been trained to think, 'What can I do? How can I fix this?'

My mum does a weekend self-help-course-thing called 'Insight'. I decide to do it, it seems like it might ... sort it all (the grief, and also me).

It's two evenings and a full weekend in a large conference room in Primrose Hill. I'm surrounded by lost souls, lovely, kind, lost souls. All sorts of lostness. They're much older, trying to find answers for all the faults and rips that have happened to them in life. I am the youngest apart from one other girl, who is sixteen and suffering very badly from what life has thrown at her. The other attendees marvel at us, the teenagers: 'How lucky we are to be finding answers now. How much our lives will change!' But we are broken girls. She is covered in self-harm scars, I am covered inside with self-hatred. We are broken girls with a future, I suppose they mean.

We talk about emotions in relation to love, joy, success, money, fear, rejection, hope — what it all means. The leader, she had cancer but now she doesn't, and she always wanted a red sports car and she thought about it and now she has one. It sounds silly, but it isn't in the room; it's a space blown up with hope, brimming with it. It reminds me of my dad. He was so hopeful. He had an energy that seemed as though it was going to go somewhere — not sure where, but it would be somewhere interesting.

I don't really talk about my grief to the group. I say: 'My dad died,' and I change the subject — to the hope, the wonderful hope. What will we do now? Now we all know who we are?

I go back to school on Monday and tell my best friend the news: 'I'm fixed! I know, I have the answers!'

'You seem so much better,' she says.

'I am,' I think, 'I'm over it!'

Finally. I'm over his death and I'm okay, it's such relief. I'm done. This grief thing is finally finished, and I can just relax and have a life now. I'm elated. It's done.

I Lit A Candle for You

I lit a candle in Poland,
In Vienna,
In the Czech Republic,
In Brazil,
In Rome,
In Venice,
In Verona (lots of choice in the Catholic countries).
I lit a candle at a shrine in India,
I lit one at the cathedral in Paris,
In a plain church in Norway,
In a small church in Sweden,

In London, in the church we had your funeral in,
In churches built on top of Saxon burial grounds and
Roman temples,
In Christopher Wren's Gothic offerings all over the
City, I lit them.
In Spain,
In Liverpool,
In Hungry,
In Tunisia,
In New York, I lit them. Small white wax candles.

I paid 20p, 50p, €1, $1, 1 diram, I put what coins I had in the offering, and I lit the flame from the other candles, the other memories.

I pushed it into the holder tightly. I pushed it in so that you wouldn't dare move.
I lit them for you. To say, 'He was here. He was bloody here.'

These candles go out, but they were here, I know because I lit them.

3

Modern Mourning

How Are We Grieving Now?

Where are we now with grief? How does grief fit into our digital world? Has it been changed by the vastness of the internet, by the myriad ways that we have of capturing and recording someone's likeness, or by the fact that a social media profile can still live after they have gone? What does it mean to grieve for someone in the age of death trolls, Facebook memorials, and Kanye creating a hologram of Kim's dead dad as a gift of love?[1]

I started becoming aware of this new world of grief through my podcast, the *Griefcast*. Digital grievers (as I describe them) would casually invite me to look at their phone screen in order to show me their dead person's photo as if this were normal. I say this as only I, an analogue griever, can. My dad died in 1998, before the internet was the world we lived in, five months before Google was created, six years before Facebook, seven years before YouTube. We have moved to a new planet he never even knew existed.

Officially, my year of birth classifies me as a millennial, but being born in the early 1980s means I have one foot in the metaverse and another in the loud, clunky planet of dial-up modems. I remember life before social media, I remember being blown away at the concept of wireless internet (walking around my house with a laptop shouting, 'I can still get it in here!'). I'm a twentieth-century relic. I was born into the world of VHS, cassette tapes and

---

[1] If you don't know what I'm talking about, watch it, because it's too weird to describe.

handwritten letters. My grief is not stored in the digital sphere. For me, the objects and memories that keep my dad present only have a physical presence — a glass mushroom he bought me on holiday, a Polaroid of me on his shoulders, a landline phone bill with 'Let's Discuss! Dad x', with his large swooping Ds, written in felt-tip pen. My grief is old-fashioned, mechanical, outdated. If you google my dad's name, nothing comes up.

I did it again as I wrote this, to check. I doubted myself. Maybe he'll be there in the other world we all live in now? … But no. His life and my grief are contained in analogue memories. Anything I do have that is digital is there because it has been transferred from its analogue original, and still has its date stamp in red numbers in the right-hand corner to prove it. He has no home in the digital world. I can't read his texts or listen to voicemails. His voice is a foreign country; they record things differently there.

I had no idea how quaint my analogue memories were until I started talking to digital grievers and they described their wealth of memory options. I realised how much had changed since he had died; how many places we now have in which to hoard our memories of the dead. These digital grievers didn't have to commit every scrap and relic of that person to memory — they had a backup drive, or even just a phone with a 32GB memory. In the small machine that they carried with them everywhere, they could keep messages, emails, texts, WhatsApps, voice notes, photos, videos, social media profiles, websites. The internet was holding infinite fragments of their person. They may have shared their grief journey on a dedicated website or app, allowing friends to follow and record every stage of the process; or their dead person may have written a blog, or recorded a podcast explaining how they felt about their journey to death. So many options for recollections to rest easily.

The abundance of memories available to the digital griever bewildered me. I felt like an old granny clutching onto her straw hat as a new-fangled automobile raced past, shouting into the dust as it whizzed by, 'Oh my, they go faster than horses don't they!' The digital griever had everything: their dead (seemed to me) to be accessible, available, whenever they needed them. I was profoundly and deeply jealous of this access. To still have a mobile number to ring, just to hear the voicemail, an Instagram page to visit to see them alive. What they had seemed like magic to me. They had a digital grief that I could only dream of.

If I didn't have any digital remnants to stitch together, what did I have? Somewhere in my mum's house, in the depths of the attic, in a faded and dusty cardboard box, was a VHS of my brother's eighteenth birthday. If I had made the effort to go and get a ladder, get into the attic, quietly scream at the spiders, dig out the video, eBay a VHS player, plug it in, get it to work and then pop the tape in, I could have watched it and seen my dad. I would have seen a shakily held recording, made on a 1990s camcorder, of a go-karting hangar – a hundred blue and red tyres piled up to make the venue look less like a converted warehouse off the North Circular, my teenage-adult brother and his friends lolling around in green boiler suits designed to make them feel like Formula One drivers rather than the boys they are. Every now and again I appear. I am fourteen and my hair is fluffy and brushed, because no one had told me yet not to do that to curly hair. I am smiley, excited to be there, with these big-boy-small-adults. The camera pans across the track, go-karts racing, bashing into each other; shots of some of the boys drinking beer, trying to appear relaxed, but obviously excited about this break from the normality of suburban London. In the background, my dad appears, jet black hair on a receding hairline, looking out onto the track. He doesn't act up for the camera; he isn't larking about. He's watching the races and smiling. Sometimes he's racing against the boys and not giving them any leeway. As the session ends, they have a winner's ceremony, reading out the fastest scores, and my dad wins. He takes first place on a small winner's podium, next to my brother standing on the second-place platform. A man who has been driving since he was seventeen has decided to beat his son on his birthday.[2] They give my dad a bottle of cheap champagne and he shakes it up all over them. There is laughing and banter, a language I don't quite understand. My dad was often embarrassing at events that involved our friends; he firmly believed his job as a parent (and, it seemed to me, his purpose in life) was to embarrass his children. Except my brother and I didn't laugh it off. We really cringed when he did it. But that day he was behaving himself with the boys, he wasn't playing up. He seemed relaxed. I think that day, his teenage-boy-self felt happy.

---

[2] In case you were wondering how competitive my family is and why I'm not allowed to play Monopoly any more.

I know this is what I would have seen because eventually I did go up into the attic and reclaim the VHS. A digital transfer later and I could skip the complicated visit to the attic and just watch it on my laptop. My dad on a MacBook Air, not even plugged into an extension cord. He would have marvelled at that. Twenty years on, I watched the video and realised I remembered being there as much as I remembered the video itself. I had watched it as a teenager, soon after he'd died. I'd found it next to the TV and, before I knew what I was doing, I had put it on and pressed play. It was painful, heart-wrenching even, to see him there on the screen, knowing I couldn't see him in reality any more. It felt almost ghoulish. I watched it again a year or so later when, clearing up videos of *Red Dwarf* and *Blackadder*, I noticed his familiar writing in pencil on a video's white label. After that, he and it got put away. I didn't want to stumble on it any more. But it turns out that I had committed it so strongly to memory that I could simply replay it in my head when I needed to. I had internalised every detail of that video because it was all I had if I wanted to see him alive again: him, and me, grief-free and frizzy-haired.

At first, I felt jealous of the digital grievers, especially when comparing my analogue scrapbook of memories to theirs: the bile-pit feeling that is made even more extreme in grief – when it feels like someone else had *more* – *more* time, *more* care, *more* hope, *more* luck – *more* memories. But as that feeling waned, I could see that what I was really feeling was sadness, a sense of loss at not having the kind of memories that the digital world allowed.

One of the many laments I have for my dad is that he never truly experienced the digital age – he would have bloody loved it. He was obsessed with communication. He set up an intranet in our house so he, my brother and I could message each other in a sort of prototype version of MSN. (We didn't use it much, we stuck to shouting: 'TEA'S READY,' and huffing that we hadn't been heard.) He had a pager, a car phone, a PalmPilot and these weird hexagon-shaped magnets that stuck to a whiteboard, which you could use to brainstorm ideas (this memory stayed with me because he woke me up one night to show them to me, as if I, a sleepy ten-year-old in a teddy-bear nightie, was going to start strategising with him). If he'd encountered WhatsApp, he might have genuinely exploded. I can say with absolute confidence that had he lived past 2000, he would have been the idiot queuing for every new iPhone. He would have had an Instagram and a Twitter. LinkedIn would have seemed a genuinely fun place to him.

But he didn't make it to the millennium and so I have the clunky analogue versions of our lives. I have to imagine myself sat atop his shoulders, him beaming in his 'World Runners' jumper, because the Polaroid that captured this moment has faded so badly that I took it down from my noticeboard – I couldn't bear to see it disappearing, deteriorating, as physical objects will insist on doing. Another loss, another grief. Sometimes I find the old BT phone bill he wrote me a note on and just look at it. And I remember that we used to talk and communicate about household things, nothing special – just that I was his daughter and I used the phone too much. It seems like nothing, but sometimes I think the banality of it makes it more powerful than anything the digital age could offer.

I do believe that because my grief is rooted in the mess of an analogue world that there are fewer opportunities for me to be stung by things that remind me of him. If I want to find him, if I want to open the wound, it involves time, effort and a lot of (actual) dust. I write this to reassure my analogue friends that there are advantages to our plight. And, of course, our memories are no less valid for their antiquity. Memories do not need to be HD, virtual or 4K quality to matter. The objects you hold dear, the fragments you have gathered of your dead person, are worthy of your love and appreciation. Sometimes referred to as 'transitional objects within grief', they come to mean more to us during the process of grieving. Our person is somehow contained in them, just as a child has a blanket to remind them they are safe. Tiny things can hold love, a childhood, a time before death was part of your vocabulary. I still have the glass mushroom he gave me when I was a child – green-teal glass with a rainbow swirl like a slick of oil on top of it. Turkey? Malta? I remember going into the shop, a day trip from our package holiday hotel. I remember seeing it among the many shelves of tourist glass and thinking it was the most beautiful thing I'd ever seen, and then telling him this. He offered to buy it. He was listening to me, focussed for once, and he bought it for me. I felt overwhelmed: now I owned the most beautiful thing in the world. It sits on my desk today, reminding me: you had a dad and you were loved. The longer I have grieved, the more I realise so many of the memories are just that: a reminder that you were loved and that you loved in return, in whatever complicated way that was expressed. The things I do have could probably fit into one cardboard box – just enough to hold the memory of a dead dad after twenty years. Not much, but, if I'm honest, it's enough.

REVEREND RICHARD COLES

There's this awful fear you have that they will fade away and you won't remember their voice or their walk ... David loved eau de Cologne and could have had a duty-free shop and, after he died, I kept finding bottle after bottle. So it's on a shelf in my bathroom now and I have a squirt of one of his colognes before I go to bed and there's something about the pungency of that and also the fade of that, that helps me.

All I could see with digital grief was the wondrous abundance. But after speaking to digital grievers, I began to see the naivety of viewing more as better. The voice notes, the emails, the profile pages, didn't heal the grief. The person was still gone. Grief is still present with likes, Reels and superfast broadband. As I spoke to modern griefsters, I began to understand the complications of this new world. It's hard enough to navigate social media as a living person, let alone as someone who is also grieving the dead.

NIKESH SHUKLA
Writer. Nikesh's mum died in 2010, when he was thirty.

Overnight my mum's Facebook turned into a shrine of people leaving messages. They didn't know what had happened. They didn't even know she had had cancer, because it had been two weeks. So, the day after my mum died, my sister and I had to work out how to kill her digitally, which is really hard. So we had to work out a way of shutting down her Facebook account because we felt we couldn't deal with it. While all this outpouring of emotion was great, it meant that we had to suddenly phone loads of people the day after, when we weren't necessarily ready to.

ESHAAN AKBAR
Stand-up comedian and podcaster. Eshaan's mother passed away before he began his comedy career.

I know full well that there's a part of me that's keeping my mum alive. I got signed a year after starting comedy – I had some amazing gigs, amazing opportunities, things I never imagined I'd be doing. When I heard the news I picked up my phone to go tell my mum – she's still listed in my favourites – and the fact that I still have that instantaneous reaction means that there's something I haven't quite processed.

The term 'thanatechnology' – technology's control over death and grief – was first coined by thanatologist Dr Carla Sofka back in the early 1990s.[3] She was studying how the internet was beginning to help us grieve in a new

---

[3] Thanatology, the study of dying, death, loss and grief, is named after the Greek God Thanatos, the personification of death (think less black cloak and scythe, more wings and strong arms). (Sidenote: by Roman times he looked more like Cupid, but with his legs crossed and holding a torch downwards. Grief doesn't equal love, in my opinion, but an upside-down Cupid makes a lot more sense.)

way. As we move deeper into the twenty-first century, the physical world and the digital world vie for precedence. The internet is no longer somewhere we visit occasionally; it's a place where we live, day in, day out. When someone dies, they die in the real world and in the digital one.

Soon after the journalist and writer Deborah Orr died in October 2019, Twitter deleted her account with them. Not only was her legacy of commentary on the platform gone, but the DMs between friends – years of exchanges, silly messages, records of whole digital friendships –were also obliterated: dead online as well as in life. I have previously devoured books of correspondence and letters exchanged between famous people – writers, academics – and found joy in being able to slip nosily into their thoughts. The fact that these letters have survived, that they were saved from the rubbish bin or the fire, has always seemed some sort of a miracle to me. But the saving was usually done by someone who knew the author. In the digital world we are beginning to realise how little content we own. Memories have become the property of the particular platform on which they were published; if they are removed, there's often very little you can do to hold on to them. How will we remember the great writers and communicators of the digital age? Will a museum exhibition simply give you the Twitter password and allow you to scroll?

The more our lives become digitally connected, the more we live on these platforms and eventually grieve on them. The death of any celebrity is quickly followed by its own Twitter hashtag – which is how many of us find out about a death these days. There's even the horror of noticing someone is trending on the sidebar, the desperate clicking just to make sure the news is that they're *not* dead. When a death is announced on social media before those who were close to the person get a chance to find out, it can be hugely shocking and painful. Dr Sofka cites an example in the United States where four high-school students were killed in a car crash. When one of their mothers arrived at the hospital emergency room not knowing the fate of her son, she was greeted by his teacher. The crash had been reported on social media and fellow students had worked out who'd been in the car by who hadn't texted them back. The names spread on social media and many people found out who had died this way, including the boy's teacher, who headed to the hospital before the mother even knew what had happened.

It's difficult to quantify if finding out in this way lessens or worsens someone's pain – but it is certainly an incredibly fast way of communicating difficult and tragic news, and one that we are still learning to navigate. Digital grief is just so new. We are not used to grieving like this and we are having to find our way by making mistakes as we go.

One of the horrors of the internet is trolling, a form of bullying that can be so severe that it has even led to people taking their own lives after suffering online abuse. An element of this dire practice is death trolling, where people make jokes, jibes and horrible comments about a person after their death. Facebook memorial pages can be taken over by death trolls mocking the appearance of the dead person and hashtags swamped with memes ridiculing the way the person died or the grief that others are sharing online. In 2011, a UK internet troll was even jailed for creating memes and YouTube videos of teenagers who had been killed in tragic circumstances.

The increase in this kind of behaviour online has led to large social media companies changing their polices when it comes to death and bereavement – policies no one originally thought might intersect with grief. Facebook made significant changes to its guidelines after a particular case in 2012. Prior to this, Facebook had allowed anyone to lock and memorialise an account simply by sending them an obituary. In the 2012 case, the mother of a fifteen-year-old girl who was killed when she was hit by a train in Germany was unable to access her daughter's account as it had already been memorialised by someone else. The mother went to court as there was a concern that the girl was being bullied at the time of the incident, and her mother wanted to see who had been messaging her daughter prior to her death. Initially, she won the case, but later an appeals court ruled in favour of the right to private data over parental rights. The parents then appealed again and the case was only overturned on the grounds that the contract the girl had had with Facebook ended when she died – a complication I imagine no one in that family foresaw when she created her account as a young teenager.

It is situations such as these that force us to look at the digital world as just that: a world. Two of my podcast guests talked about the experience of finding out via Facebook that parents had died; neither was in contact with them at the time – one was estranged from their father, the other was adopted and had only just discovered their birth mother. Both guests spoke of the shock of learning, in a place they'd normally expect to see status updates from school friends, that their parent had died. They just weren't prepared for it. Facebook was not created to do the job of a hospital waiting room, but it has become that, and more: a market square of everyone you've ever met exchanging frivolous and important information simultaneously.

Another policy change Facebook has made regarding death and grief is to allow users to nominate someone to oversee their page as a 'legacy contact', should they die. The legacy contact can choose to turn the deceased's page into a memorial page, where those who already know you can share memories and photos; or they can choose to keep it open, almost as if you were still alive, so people can continue to interact with you and even add you as a friend. If you do make the choice to nominate someone as your legacy contact, you will probably also choose to tell them that you've done so. Social media's acknowledgement of its role in our lives could therefore have the surprising consequence of making us think about what happens after our own deaths. Even beginning a conversation about legacy contacts could spark another, perhaps bigger, conversation about wills or funerals. Just allowing that thought into our digital psyche will hopefully encourage us to start thinking about our 'digital dust' – a phrase coined by the original thanatologist, Dr Sofka.

It's not known how many people have signed up to the legacy contact service, or even know about it. If, in the here and now, we can't talk about our funeral plans or end-of-life care, are we ready to admit how much digital life we might also need to administer after a death? 'It is easier to let information accumulate in our "digital external memories" than it is to bother deleting it,' cautions Professor Viktor Mayer-Schönberger, a digital data expert. 'Forgetting has become costly and difficult, while remembering is inexpensive and easy.' For many digital grievers this isn't a hypothetical: they are already having to navigate this strange new world and all its complexities.

However, definite benefits exist for the bereaved in the digital age. There is now a huge online grief community to support the new digital griever. Since I began *Griefcast* in 2016, a plethora of online social media grief accounts has been created, aiming to help people through their grief. These often offer brightly coloured graphics, easily readable and digestible slides on how to, say, talk about your grief with others, how to handle Christmas, how to handle lockdown grief, Father's Day, Mother's Day. Some simply share stories, pictures, photos, memes, doodles. Just following the hashtags #grief #griefjourney #griefandloss #griefsucks can help you access similar accounts. Every month I see the number of beautifully designed accounts, with thoughtfully presented infographics, growing and growing. Here is a community of people not afraid to talk about the feelings and fears that are affecting them. A digital griever can choose to dip in and out of this world. One Gen Z griever I spoke to said she had been navigating the internet all her life, so knowing when to leave it, including the digital grief community, was an easy choice for her. There is, of course, still a danger of boiling huge and complicated states of distress down to easily digestible slides and illustrations. Grief is not content; it is a process we learn to live with and can't be solved with just a bold font and a clashing colourway.

But the power of the digital can also heal – it can allow you to be anywhere in the world and take part in a funeral service, speak at a memorial or even say goodbye to a dying loved one. As we have seen during the Covid-19 pandemic, without technology so many final words would have been missed, adding more trauma to an already unfathomably painful situation. In 2021, the Church of England conducted an online survey which revealed that seven out of ten people who had experienced someone's death in the past year had been unable to attend the funeral, and that 40 per cent had watched the funeral online via live streaming. A Twitter post showing iPads being prepared for an intensive care unit in the US – a raft of screens on stands lined up to provide digital goodbyes – went viral in December 2020. It was a striking image of grief in the digital age and of the power technology has given us, a function no one would have predicted prior to the pandemic. We can now all log on to a Zoom and watch not only a funeral, but someone's death. You can record last words for young children to see later. You can capture a death and a time that previously would have been lost to ageing memories.

EMILY DEAN
Writer and broadcaster. Emily's sister, Rachael, and her father and mother all died within the space of three years.

Rach had to spend Christmas Day in hospital, and I thought, 'This isn't going to end well.' So, Christmas

Day, we took the girls in – and it's funny I took a video of that, because I thought for the little one, she was only eleven months old, I like that I've got that. Even though it's a bit grim and my sister's wearing hospital scrubs – all my family are there, and they're all gone now too, as my mum and dad died really soon after my sister – so it's nice for the girls to have that …

Recently I said to her older daughter, Mimi, who's fifteen now – and I was nervous about bringing it up – 'I have a video of Mummy in the hospital with you and your sister. I've been nervous about showing you, I thought you might not want to see it, it's kind of upsetting.'

But she looked at me and she said, 'I really, really want to see it.'

Emily's bravery in capturing that moment still moves me – to have been able to think straight, to have seen past the illness to the future. Sometimes the digital world can offer a lot more healing than hurt. I am so glad and grateful that today's grieving youth will have more to remember their dead by than I do, despite how precious my scraps have become to me. A life where a child can keep pressing play – on not just one video, but many recordings – can keep looking, can keep coming back to that image and asking, 'Do I look like them now? Who were they?' is part of a hopeful future.

In 2020 a dear friend died suddenly. While scrolling through my inbox I abruptly found what proved to be our last correspondence. I broke again when I saw those emails. I reread them, tracked our conversations and smiled at her writing. I was blinded by our innocence of

103

what would happen next. Then, as if they were precious letters, I left them in the inbox to be kept safe. I had never truly navigated this before, but I knew I couldn't archive them away, not yet, if only to feel like I could still scroll down and say hello. It stings when I accidentally see her name on my computer, and yet it also warms my heart, as only grief can, to remember such a beautiful person. I'm happy to keep a memory of her there, with me on my screen, and in my kitchen, where the small wooden Welsh lovespoon she gave me sits in a mug filled with pens. Every now and again I catch either digital or analogue her and remember that she was once here, and what a wonderful person she was.

NIKESH SHUKLA

There was one day where I was looking for something of my mum's and I found this shopping list that she'd written, it was like a really mundane shopping list: Weetabix, sugar, whatever, pasta. But there was something very powerful about seeing her handwriting and her handwriting involved in something as mundane as doing the big shop ... One day I was like, 'I'm going to do this shop.' So, I did my mum's shop and had all this stuff.

Then I remembered on our wedding day we'd been presented with a book of recipes – my mother-in-law had asked everyone in both of our families to basically write down a recipe of their family and she'd collated all the family recipes – so we had this family recipe book. There were two recipes from my mum in there and I was like, 'I need to make something from all this food I've bought. So, I'm going to try some Gujarati home cooking.' I tried to cook something, nearly burnt the house down, but there was this moment amongst all the smoke and the fire alarm going off, that my kitchen smelt just like Mum's kitchen, just for a second – and it really took me to another place.

Modern mourning is still just that – mourning – and although it seems to provide options that those of us grieving in the past could only have dreamt of, the fact remains that digital grief is grief. What the digital world can offer is just another place to put that grief. Because, whether you are holding on to pieces of paper or a ream of Tweets, you're still trying to hold on to the person. Digital grief certainly offers you a better quality of sound or image, but it doesn't provide you with what you really seek: them, alive. Because whether analogue or digital, what we're searching for is a way to keep them with us. That's what all of this is – a searching for them after they've gone: left with an absence and looking for a presence.

So, take these memories with you: take what you need and keep living. By allowing yourself to keep a fragment of them present – whether that's in letters squirrelled away or in voicemails forever saved – you are allowing yourself to live and to grieve at the same time. It's there and yet you must keep on living without them, however you can balance this. It's okay to do so. The joy of knowing that they are still with you in so many ways can remain, when you need to remember, when you want to remember: they were there.

They were here.

They were here.

Wave – 2001, Brighton

My mum drops me off. We unpack my boxes from the car, and it feels unreal, like watching an American film about kids going to college. My little room, a new building at the edge of the campus – there are cows outside the window. I'm excited but I've no idea what's happening. I have my dad's old cassette player to listen to my *Harry Potter* audiobook on and a guitar I can play three chords on. Oh, what's that? Yes, I am pretty cool.

She goes to leave; she goes to hug me and we suddenly both get upset. 'I won't stay, I'll cry,' she says laughing. It dawns on us both. She's going home, alone. He's not here. It's always dawning on us both. Oh, he's not here again.

People ask a lot of questions about family, and I dance around their questions. I get into a play in the autumn term and a boy in the cast asks me as if he wants the truthful answer. I say my dad is dead. He stares at me. He talks about his loss. His shoulders drop and he stares at me. I know what he's thinking, 'She gets it. She gets it.'

But I don't. I don't understand his grief. I want to. I go to his small room one day and he takes something, and we listen to the *Romeo + Juliet* soundtrack, and I feel numb. I'm fine, but he's scared me. His pain is very near the surface. I didn't know it could do that; I don't want mine to be. I need to get a hold of it and bury it so that it can't creep out when it feels like it.

I stop seeing him for tea. I feel bad and he's annoyed. But I don't know how to say, 'Your pain is too visible for me' (without sounding like a twat). So I don't say much.

Lesson learnt. Don't talk too much. Don't show anyone how bad the mess is.

A year on and I move to a small room in a house like a grown-up. My northern flatmate's northern friends come to stay one holiday – lads with a capital L, thick accents and cans of beer are suddenly all over the house. They are funny and stupid and so much fun. It all seems more like a sitcom now, I'm almost relaxed around them. Then one of them starts doing 'Your Mum' jokes. They all pile on, more and more awful jokes, one after the other; they are howling with laughter at how disgusting they can be. I bristle. The more they see my reaction, the more they tease me. I try to speak to the one I'm snogging (everyone got one boy to snog, so it was fair). I say, 'She's all I've got, don't you understand? I can't take the jokes because I don't have anything left.'

He's kind but confused. He tells them to lay off me, but they don't. 'It's jokes!' they say again and again. 'Just a joke Cariad.' Why can't I laugh at this? No one looks at me knowing. No one understands what I mean when I say that I have so little left.

This is why I have to be careful. If you leave your feelings on the floor people can step on them. Pack them away more carefully. Don't talk about it to those who don't get it. Don't talk about it to those who are in pain. Be careful with the grief, Cariad. Wrap it up and put it back carefully.

Years later I am a mother, a writer, finally in therapy. The northern boy I was snogging has become a friend, our past an embarrassing and distant memory. We're grown-ups now and he is very sick. I send him a card because I want to say, I'm sorry, you don't deserve this. We meet and talk and he's as funny and silly as he was then, even with cancer. He apologises. I know what he's thinking, he gets it. 'We didn't know,' he says. 'We didn't know what you meant; we had no idea.' A small muscle in my back eases. I was right, they didn't know. I was allowed to be sensitive.

Tell Past Cariad, run back and tell her. Shout it through the years, 'This is shit! It's really hard!' But then I felt stupid, embarrassed, ashamed of it. Of all the mess I kept in, that kept leaking everywhere. Pain all over the floor, like I'd wet myself. Wishing I knew how to control myself, this mess, this grief. Ugh, this grief.

Things I Don't Do Because You Died

Go hang-gliding (Mum makes me promise)
Go to bed on an argument
Leave without saying goodbye (to everyone in case they
die, or I die)
Take drugs
Get too drunk
Buy Father's Day cards
Take middle-aged men very seriously
Cope well when middle-aged men ignore me
Appreciate being told what to do by middle-aged men
Ring you up and ask how something works
Have my grammar corrected
Feel embarrassed by how unembarrassed you were of
yourself
Argue with you
Know you
Trust that everything will be fine.

Wave – 2002, Brighton

I am sat at the shore, staring at waves. Literal waves of grief coming at me endlessly and infuriatingly, over and over again. I stare at them. How dare they? How small I am. How little I matter against the actual background of the earth. A smudge, a dot, a tiny person shouting at the waves.

I'm in the throes of something so awful and I don't really remember how I got here.

It's raining, not properly. The air is full of damp and my hair frizzes into a tangled wire-wool mess. I am holding a white umbrella that lets the light in but today there's only grey gloom. The sky seems to vibrate with it.

I tramp down the ridiculously rocky beach. I sit by the weird wooden fence that splits the beach up into tiny chunks of rocky squares. I throw stones as hard as I can, but I'm shit at it. They don't go far enough, or they just plop in the water. I don't want a comic plop; I want my fist to become a huge mallet that punches the sea so hard that it sends tsunamis along to Eastbourne. I want the earth to know I'm not okay with this. I'm shouting. I hear myself before I know it's me. There's no one around, but I recognise quietly I'm not okay because I'm shouting at the sea and that's a bit mad, isn't it? I shout out loud. 'Where are you? ... Where the fuck are you?'

I'm sobbing. I pull the umbrella down onto my head, so I must look like a tiny weeping mushroom. Still the drizzle gets underneath and the rain and the tears on my face blur into one. Even as I write this, the memory blurs like ink spreading across a wet page. I have a terrible pain that is stitched into my gut at that moment. It's very probably the start of the IBS I have for the next twenty years. I ache and cry until eventually I stop. There aren't any more tears, I can't squeeze out any more. My throat hurts. I feel stupid as I hear the last honking noises I'm making. No one sees me, the beach is too wet for other visitors.

I feel numb, like I've been sick and thrown something up. I leave it behind on the beach, let the waves take it. They can have all my pain and shouting; they can gobble it all up and drag it down to the bottom of the sea.

I walk back up the hill to my flat. On the way I bump into someone I know. 'Ah hello! How are you?' they say all jolly.

I smile. 'Hey! Ah, yeah, I'm great thanks!'

What a lie. What a performance. I'm laughing and exchanging words about the rain, and I march off waving, my hands still shaking.

4

Personalise Your Grief

Who Were You When it Happened?

'And the past is the past and that is what time means,
and time itself is one more name for death ... '

C. S. *Lewis,* A Grief Observed

Hendon, 1998. Already a depressing prospect. My mum
has found me a young person's grief counsellor and they've
offered me a session. I'm not enthusiastic. I'm as willing as
a barnacle being politely asked to leave the hull of a boat.
'Just go once,' she says. 'You don't have to go again if you
don't like it.'

She waits in the car and gives me a smile, willing me in
as I grumpily slam the car door. You can hear me thinking
'This'll be shit' just by looking at me.

The building itself is totally brown. The roof is brown,
the walls are brown, the bricks of the building are brown.
Thatcher-era bricks, thin and sad – the antithesis of the cosy,
homely red bricks of old London. Inside, the wall colours
switch to beige. I head to an institutional-looking reception
area, where the chairs are covered with an oddly itchy, dark
brown material. It's flecked all over, giving the impression
it's covered in fluff. I feel compelled to brush it down.

This place, this building, this session, is my gap. The gap
I have fallen into because I am fifteen. If my dad had
waited just a few months longer to die,[1] I would have been
sixteen and would have qualified for adult bereavement

---

[1] Rude.

counselling. In the late 1990s there weren't a lot of grief services for people classed as children. Thankfully, it is now a very different picture. Today there are specialist children's bereavement charities, picture books, speakers, TED talks, podcasts — an array of services available to help children deal with death, a network to catch you if you want to be caught. But in 1998 there was no internet, no way to reach out to others. We had word of mouth, whispered rumours that Rebecca in Class 11SJ's dad had also died (but she wouldn't talk about it). Finding others was hard. But there was at least Hendon and my brilliant mum trying to find something for me to hold on to, even as she was drowning in her own sorrow.

I am here, in the brown building off a dual carriageway, to talk to a lady about what's happened to me. Except, obviously, I don't want to talk to her. I am fifteen. I don't want to do anything that makes me vulnerable. I want to tell her to fuck off, and go and smoke twenty B&H Gold cigarettes.[2]

The lady is nice, and she has that therapy voice that grates but also makes you relax. We go into a room, and she asks me to sit down on a tiny chair. It's comically tiny because it's for a child. An actual child. I'm small, but I'm not the size of an eight-year-old. I sit down and my knees are in my face. She joins me on a matching tiny chair, so now we both have knees in our faces. This, I feel, is unnecessary. I know I'm classed as a child in this land, but she isn't. It's a gesture of solidarity, I realise, but it only

---

[2] In the old days, before vapes, we just smoked cigarettes. More nicotine, less fruity smells. Would not recommend it now.

strengthens my resolve: I do not belong here. Between us is a similarly tiny table with a doll's house on it. Next to it are crappy colouring pencils and, around the room, sad, wooden, educational toys (brown, of course, grubby from use by other sad children). The air feels unthreatening, devoid of either joy or sadness. I know that this is a trick. That's how they get you. They want to lull you into being emotional by being so dull that you have to cry just to remind yourself that you're alive.

I'm ready to win this battle. I know it's a battle because I've heard them say that he 'battled' cancer, or even that he lost his 'fight'. These days I'd judge this grossly insensitive language – a reductive way to talk about terminal illness – but fifteen-year-old me has absorbed it and is now, *Street Fighter*-style, ready to fight grief. One beige room and a sad wooden play kitchen will not defeat my armoury, even if the therapist is trained for such teenage fortifications.

First, she tries the 'being silent' therapy trick. It's awful, excruciating. I shuffle in my tiny seat. But then she speaks (I judge this as a sign of weakness) and asks me a question. How am I feeling today? Oh, I can deal with this. Cariad 1, Nice Lady 0.

I'm used to questions. That's easy. I've learnt how to be aggressive enough to make it seem not worth the bother and yet eloquent enough to make it sound like I'm fine. I say, 'I don't want to be here.'

And she says, 'That's fine.'

That throws me. I'm expecting to be told off, so I can tell someone to fuck off (because, irritatingly, my dad has died and I can't say that to him any more). She carries on asking questions. 'How have I been?' … 'How is school?' …

I mumble, I'm vague, convinced that she won't be able to gather anything from this meeting other than I should probably go home. Of course, she's well trained, because soon she brings out the cavalry: a surprise question. She asks me if I've dreamt of him. (Cariad 1, Nice Lady 1.) I have. How does she know that? Is that normal? Am I doing something wrong? So many questions I wish I could ask, but my mouth won't let me form the words. *Breathe.* You can tell her without giving anything away.

'Yes, I have.'

I'm determined to leave it at that, but suddenly more details tumble out – like I've opened the washing-machine door and socks are jumping out at her to be chosen to get hung on the dryer. Suddenly, I'm talking to her – about when my brother dreamt of him and he was bathed in light and said something nice, and when my mum dreamt of him, and he was floating and told her he was okay. When I dreamt of him, I saw his dead body, yellowed and stiff, still wearing the green sweatshirt he wore when he was sick. His body was in the porch by the front door, and we kept walking past it to go to school and saying, 'God, we need to do something about that … '

'I didn't get a message or white light. Am I doing something wrong? – ' I stop myself. Shit. (Cariad 1, Nice Lady 2.)

I haven't told anyone about this dream because it makes me feel awful. Terribly, terribly guilty. I must be grieving wrong. I'm not getting any angel visits, just hygiene-anxiety dreams. She's kind, she says, 'Perhaps you're dealing with it more practically? Perhaps that's how you're coping.'

And then an odd sensation happens: I feel better. I feel relieved that I told her and that she didn't laugh or judge. I almost relax.

Then I sense she's pleased, she can see it has helped. I panic, that's enough. I've let a wall down and I'm terrified more will spill out from behind it.

In reality, I'm desperate to talk to her, to anyone, longing for someone to say, 'You have to go to this place every week, you have to talk about it, we're making you, this is what you have to do because you need it, you will be helped.' I want someone to make the decision for me. Instead, I sit here pretending to be an adult in the children's room, and I tell her I don't want to come back. It's not for me. I don't need it.

She says that's fine. She's calm. She lets me go. I walk slowly out of the room, wondering if she'll shout after me and say I must return. Nope, my performance of 'Teenage Girl who's grieving but is actually dandy, thank you very much' has been accepted. I didn't realise I had to want to talk about it, that it would never work to make someone face their grief without being ready. I didn't realise that she saw a scared child who needed more time and very kindly let me go and find my way by myself. I didn't fool her, or anyone. (Cariad 2, Nice Lady 3.)

I get into my mum's red Nissan Micra, with the numberplate that, oddly, has his initials at its end. 'How was it?' she says.

'Awful,' I say. I proceed to mock the nice lady who sits on tiny chairs and the room and the toys and then I explain I'm never going again. 'I tried. It was stupid. Counselling isn't for me.' Checkmate, full time, game over, I'm fine. I've got this, I'm dealing with it myself. Like a grown-up should.

I didn't go to any sort of grief therapy again for another fifteen years.

It wasn't anyone's fault. No one won or lost really. But now I look back (thanks to many years of adult therapy), and I see the child me, the girl not able to understand her grief yet. What good would making me talk have done? I had to want to talk about my grief, not be coerced into it. At fifteen, I didn't have the vocabulary to explain to someone else what was happening, let alone myself. Adolescence is a difficult phase for anyone; adding death into that mix makes it exquisitely tricky. I could cry and I could wail to my family or to friends I trusted, but it would take many more years before I was able to deconstruct what had happened, before the shock faded enough to see the damage. Everyone did their best, considering the circumstances: me, my mum, the nice lady. Sometimes it's just too early to verbalise the pain.

Dealing with the constraints and emotional confusion of being a teenager and then having those challenges compounded by grief was incredibly hard. But for years I chose to dismiss the age I was when my dad died – desperate to convince myself (and everyone else) that your dad dying when you're fifteen is not such a big deal. That it would have been just the same if I'd been twenty-five or thirty-two – just a dad, right? But it did matter. Because he died when I wasn't yet a fully formed person. I wasn't an adult; I wasn't a child. I wasn't finished. I was mid-conversation, both with myself and with him. I was profoundly affected by my grief, and my grief was affected by my age, in turn. That teenage me shaped and contained my grief for a long time: my unfinished-ness defined it. It was an angry, fearful, confused grief at first, because that's who I was then. My teenageness became meshed into the DNA of my grief.

This isn't just an adolescent privilege. Your grief could be wrapped up in many things: becoming an adult, being middle-aged, being elderly, becoming a parent. When you are ready to start looking at your grief – and that may be many years after the death has happened – can you ask yourself who you were then? What was shaping you at that point? There's a strong chance that there were factors in your life at that time that shaped the grief. That's okay, it's not wrong or right – those value judgements never apply to grief – but if you can see what shaped it, you can start to see what parts of you may still be hurting. Whether you had just moved out of home, just become pregnant, hadn't spoken with them for years. Can you acknowledge that you were in this specific space when grief crashed in?

STEPHEN MANGAN

The feelings come out in fits and starts and I think that's what happens: you don't just sit down and unleash all that you feel and all your pain. You don't even realise what it is sometimes for years. You don't know the effect it's had on you, how it's changed you, or damaged you or altered you. It takes a long time for that stuff to come out and it comes out in fits and starts and sudden realisations and bits of denial.

If you are in the TGC (Teenage Grief Club[3]) my tale of stunted therapy may be a familiar story to you. For years I thought I'd dealt with my grief rather badly, embarrassingly so. It wasn't until I talked to others who had also been

[3] Repping death-anxiety and nightmares since before we could vote!

bereaved as children or young adults that I realised my own reaction wasn't stupid/insane/unhelpful/irresponsible. It was pleasingly normal. One terrible counselling session and from then on in, self-medication – drunken chats, late-night confessions, a refusal to seek any professional help. It all felt very unhealthy, lonely and deeply sad at the time. But now I see I wasn't equipped for any other way of doing it. I was privileged enough to have a family I could talk to if I wanted, but I found it difficult to verbalise my feelings even to them. We did talk – about what had happened, about what it meant, who he was. But as anyone in the club will know, there is a difference between the grief you can express within your family and the grief hidden inside that doesn't have words. I was lucky enough to have support, and still I found myself flailing. As the years rolled on, I began to realise how I couldn't see my grief as a whole until I acknowledged how profoundly it had been affected by my age.

I saw later that my grief journey[4] was very typical, especially for those with circumstances that matched mine (teenage, cancer, quick diagnosis-to-death). It is not uncommon for young people who are bereaved as children/teenagers to not be able to address their grief again until they reach their thirties. We spend our childhood or teens in shock, and our twenties trying to negotiate living with it/ignoring it/making terrible mistakes. By the time we get to our thirties, we can (hopefully) look back and realise, 'Oh, a

---

[4] Every time I say 'grief journey' please accept my apologies and try to imagine a sunset, ripples lightly reflected on the calm sea, and an awful handwriting font telling you to: 'Follow your grief and you'll find your love.' I am not a fan of the grief meme – unless you count the one I made of Oprah, arms outstretched, saying: 'Congratulations, it's the anniversary and you got dressed!' which we can't use because we don't have the budget.

lot of this pain is probably about what happened to me back then. I wonder if I can do something about that?'

JOEL GOLBY
Writer and journalist. Joel's dad died when he was a teenager and his mum died when he was twenty-five.

I think I didn't realise that I wasn't coping very well. I thought I was smashing it. I was like, 'I am so fucking good at having a dead mum – I am crushing this.' And then one day, about two years later, I realised that I hadn't smashed it and I hadn't confronted it – I'd just sort of let it wash over me.

I'm not saying teenage grief is harder than a twenty-five-year-old's grief or a thirty-two-year-old's grief, but I want to acknowledge that the younger you are when your grief begins, the longer you take part in the process. I've carried my grief longer than many others, but that doesn't mean my experience is less or more painful. I have learnt to see that we are all in a huge club, to see not only how big it is, but how many rooms it has. Whatever shape your grief takes I think it's useful to understand the weird and bizarre limitations of your room and all the rooms you are connected to.

We all have tiny Venn diagrams we can share with each other. I am in the TGC, I am in the pancreatic cancer room, I am in the cancer section ('quick death after diagnosis', which is next to the 'more time but slow deterioration' room). We have many new rooms now – a Covid-19 room, a room of death during a pandemic, a room of quarantine grief, a room where rituals and goodbyes were distanced, masked and FaceTimed. We are linked and connected by our grief in myriad ways, sometimes helpful, sometimes envy-inducing, but we're always on the same side. If we can understand the specifics of some of these rooms, the dimensions, joys and limitations of each of them, we can better understand our grief.

We often judge our own grief harshly because we don't talk to those who share our specific grief experiences, those who can understand and empathise specifically. I have found it incredibly healing to speak to those who understood how rapidly pancreatic cancer can take someone, or those who also know what it's like to grow up too quickly as a teenager. It's healing to know that others have carried pain like yours.

Who were you when it happened? How old were you? What was happening to you at that time? Who was this person who grief descended on? It can be helpful to start by asking yourself what aspect of your pain you are minimising. For me, it was my age. For years, after walking away from that counselling session and turning it into a stupid story, I thought I had chosen not to talk about the grief. The truth was, I was unable to.

JESS MILLS
Singer, writer and podcaster. In 2018 Jess's mum, former MP Baroness Tessa Jowell, died of a brain tumour, just after Jess became a mother for the first time.

The thing that was the most intense agony for me about mum getting ill and then dying when she did, was that it intersected directly with me becoming a mother. So, my daughter was born on 28 February,

Mum was diagnosed on 24 May, and then the first year of me becoming a mother was basically overlaid with me losing my mum. I never could have anticipated how intensely I needed my mum through being a mum myself, and the experience of being mothered by her as a new mother myself were some of the most precious, treasured times of my life.

JAMES O'BRIEN
Radio host and writer. James's very good friend, Andy, died of a brain tumour in 2020.

I lost a really good friend at the age of fifty, December of 2020, at the end of lockdown ... I'm fifty in January. This is the first time [anyone] from my own peer group has passed away ... You expect to outlive your parents. I don't know I if expected to outlive my mate, Andy.

AMANDA PALMER
Singer and writer. Amanda spoke to me about her experiences with grief.

Grief will wait gently. I feel like there are relationships that I broke off, or were broken off for me, twenty to twenty-five years ago that I'm still grieving. But it's like this soft, undulating grief that's like, 'Yeah I'm not going anywhere, I'm still here but I'll wait, I'll abide, I'll be this abiding grief that will hang out gently until you're finally at the point of maturity where you can deal with what you lost, what you did, what you missed, what you fucked up.' And I also feel like the older I get, the softer all those things become – my own ability to forgive myself ...

As I pulled on this thread further, I realised that it wasn't just the age of the griefster that was important, but the emotional vocabulary they had available to them at the time. Being fifteen meant I was unable to process what had happened until I was older. It meant that for many years I lived with a grief I didn't understand. This was confusing and difficult because it meant my pain felt illogical. Much of my grief was about having a pain I couldn't articulate. I needed to figure out the type of knot I was dealing with before I could untie it.

Your knot will be different. Maybe you were older, but you had a long and difficult relationship with the person who died, in which case your grief may be wrapped up in a pain that you were never able to communicate to them when they were alive. Or maybe you had to move home immediately after the death, the home you knew them in, and that's where a lot of the grief formed – in mourning that house, that safe space. Maybe there was a family falling-out after the death, which has led to you not communicating with loved ones, so, as well as the grief around the death, there is now grief for the loss of the old support network.

There are so many situations where other losses may be felt on top of the grief. These, the other things that surround the actual pain of them not being there, can be referred to as secondary losses, or secondary grief.[5] It could be becoming a mother as you lose your own, moving house as you sell your childhood home, breaking up with a long-term

---

[5] The brilliant website 'What's Your Grief' (https://whatsyourgrief.com) has some great pictogram examples.

partner after your sibling has died. There are other pains we must negotiate on top of the pain of the person being gone. I never fully acknowledged until many years later that I lost my adolescence and part of my childhood. I lost the ability to run around, get drunk, not care what happened to me – because I became acutely aware that death can appear at any time. I found it hard to admit there was grief for the loss of being a carefree teenager, as well as for loss of a father. It seemed so frivolous to be sad about the other things – but the other things make up part of the grief.

FELIX WHITE
Musician, podcaster and writer. Felix's mum died of MS when he was seventeen.

There are elements of me that are still a seventeen-year-old ... I've got a record label and we do these bi-monthly nights which are amazing. It was my birthday in September, and they got a cake for one of these nights, and there was this big, packed smoking area and I just thought, 'I'm gonna turn around and throw this cake into this crowd, on my thirty-fourth birthday.' I thought about it, and I thought, 'These are repressed acts of being a teenager that are desperate to come out occasionally, without my will, that kid that didn't get to throw cakes around when he was seventeen ...'

Suddenly I thought, 'I'm going to throw that.' And I did.

Another helpful term to know about is 'delayed grief'. In delayed grief, your grief is put aside, sometimes for years, because of something you have to urgently deal with around the time of the death. This can happen to any griever for a variety of reasons, but especially if the death is a shock or there are tragic circumstances around it, or other things that simply must be dealt with immediately – debts, new babies, another death, severe illness. The grief can overwhelm you at any age. For young grievers, there isn't a grown-up problem to attach the delay to: the growing up bit *is* the problem.

These terms, secondary grief, delayed grief, can't fix the grief (remember we're not here to fix or remove it but to understand it) but knowing them can help you with your grief-mess, help lighten it. The reason you feel numb? You had to deal with something so huge after the death that you haven't been able to process the grief yet. Maybe you were pregnant when your parent died and attending to a new person who needed you. Bursting into tears over a cat's death eighteen months after a grandparent? The grief has waited and is now pouring out over this secondary loss: a reminder that what you're experiencing is normal. If you had to care for another elderly parent at the same time, you may feel detached, as though the grief went away – and that's okay, it did. It's no one's fault. That's just how grief works. It's waiting for a better time, when you're ready to feel those feelings.

MARIAN KEYES
Author. Marian's dad died when she was in her fifties.

Grief rearranges reality. It rearranges everything, my thoughts about existence. Everything is ordered and I don't think it can go back to the way it was before.

Like, it shouldn't: we've been given an insight into something that we couldn't understand before.

My grief waited for me. It leaked out in drips along the way, but I would hurriedly tidy up the mess when it did. When I was ready to properly face it — equipped with emotional maturity (and a brilliant therapist) — I did so. I don't regret waiting. I didn't really have a choice. That's what my grief needed to do.

What does your grief need? Is it ready to be explored? Does it need more time before you can describe it? Every grief is as different and unique as the relationship you had with the person who died. Celebrate the uniqueness if you can. It's not a negative, it's just how it is, it's what made up your relationship with them.

JILL HALFPENNY
Actress. Jill's dad died when she was six years old.

As far as I'm concerned, when people say, 'My parent died when I was young and, to be honest, it didn't really affect me,' that sort of sends my mind into a spin, because of course it did. It's one of the biggest traumas you could possibly experience as a child. But what you might have done, which is what I did, is just push it so far down that it just goes all the way down, and then it starts to manifest itself in different behaviours — like I was an anxious kid, I was a fearful kid.

SUSAN WOKOMA

Actor and writer. Susan's dad died when she was in her early twenties.

The other thing that I found really difficult as well was being twenty-four, and it happening – because I was still really young, but I was an adult … Looking back, as I get older, I realise I was swimming, drowning in it, and I didn't know what I was doing. But then I was like, 'Right, so I have this boyfriend and I live in this flat and I've told my dad I'm going to be independent with work. It's fine, I'll show you.'

So, I'm trying to do that, and I haven't borrowed a penny off him, I'm doing all the independent things … and then I lose my dad and I feel like a child again, but I'm an adult.

Your grief-mess is a part of you, a part of your life and circumstances. Your age, your culture, your religion, your economic circumstances – there'll be a collection of factors that will influence how you grieve, whether it will happen immediately or wait, whether it will be loud and emotional or you will find it difficult to talk about. When we treat grief as a one-size-fits-all, we do ourselves a huge disservice. Your grief is yours, the relationship you had with that person was yours. It's okay to investigate that grief to find out what you need.

When I finally faced my adolescent grief, I saw not what I had feared – a frightening, unwilling mess – but quite the opposite: a calm sadness. Whatever your grief-mess looks like, trust that when you are ready, you will be able to look at it. You may need a professional to hold your hand as you do so, you may need time, but you can do it. See it truthfully and you will start to understand it, you will know what it needs, and you will find a new way to carry it. You will see how, like a tree in rocky ground, you have learnt to grow your roots around it. You will hold yourself up eventually.

PHILIPPA PERRY

When we're two people together and we're in a relationship with each other, be that a significant other relationship or a mere friendship, if somebody goes, they take with them a sort of part of you and that becomes a void in you. Like your shared jokes, your shared history, the moments that just you and they had together. Your shared memories. It's like losing a part of yourself, and for a moment I think grief really hurts. Part of the reason grief really hurts is because of that void, and that hole in you. But over time other things do fill it up.

If you are reading this chapter and the idea of grief ever finding a place of peace in your life seems improbable, nay impossible, a new idea may be interesting to you: complicated grief (also known as prolonged grief disorder (PGD), or persistent complex bereavement disorder).

Complicated grief is a relatively recent and somewhat controversial discovery. It was only included in the World Health Organization's International Classification of Diseases a few years ago and in the *DSM* (*Diagnostic and Statistical Manual of Mental Disorders*, essentially the official psychiatry Bible) in 2021. Some still believe that grief is too difficult and nuanced a process to be categorised as a disorder.

This type of grief seems impossible to recover from. The idea of being okay, even years later, may seem utterly hopeless. It is estimated that between 5 and 7 per cent of people experiencing grief are experiencing complicated grief. It may occur for a variety of reasons – a very traumatic death, a history of PTSD, anxiety, traumatic childhood events, extreme dependency on the person who died, emotionally or financially – or just because. It can often be misdiagnosed as depression because it matches the feeling of life being dulled and pointless but, unlike depression, it stems entirely from a grief that seems ungetoverable. Dr Kathy Shear, founding director of the Center of Complicated Grief at the Columbia University School of Social Work, says it differs from depression in that it is a 'yearning and longing for the person who died and preoccupation with thought and memories of them; it's very centred on the person who died and really wanting them back'.

Even if your grief has been agony, most people can acknowledge that, as the years go by, there are days when it feels better/easier/lighter, there are times when they can see the end of the tunnel, feel happiness or even acknowledge that their life is growing around a very painful experience. With complicated grief, the grief can feel as raw as it did when the death happened. There doesn't seem to be a softening of the pain. It may be hard or impossible to build any new life at all. 'As we adapt,' says Dr Shear, 'grief will naturally subside and move into the background and that is what we think is different in prolonged grief disorder, that doesn't happen. We think the basic problem is that the person isn't finding that way to adapt to the loss.'

Dr Shear and others, including Holly Prigerson, professor of geriatrics, sociology and medicine, and director of the Cornell Center for Research on End-of-life Care, are working to understand this type of grief better. Dr Prigerson has devised the inventory of complicated grief – a hugely impactful change, as it means the disorder can be treated, and insurance companies will pay for treatment. When I spoke to Dr Prigerson for the BBC Radio 4 documentary *What We've Learnt About Grief*, she outlined the many repercussions of not taking prolonged grief seriously. 'The core, cardinal symptom of PGD is yearning. You're protesting, "No, I need this person back in my life,"' she explained. 'And do people feel that after someone they love, or a significant other has died? Yes, they do, but not after twelve months. If you feel that intensely all day every day, that's not normal … the long and short of it is, it doesn't matter how you get to being high on these seemingly benign symptoms, you are at significant risk of not resolving symptoms and having even physical health consequences.'

Complicated/prolonged grief is relatively rare and not what happens to most people who suffer a bereavement. However, if you feel like this, there are therapies out there – developing ones certainly, but I have spoken to those who have found this way of 'treating' grief to be life-changing. There are others who feel that categorising an emotional state such as grief in this way is a quick path to medicalising it – with the attendant fears that anti-depressants will simply be handed out – rather than someone being allowed to be sad, because someone has died. It's a complex argument, but I can only advise that you seek support that works for your grief.

*

TGC Coda

I want to speak to the Teenage Grief Club (TGC) for a moment. But please stay even if that isn't you, we can all learn from each other's stories.

Most of the writing on grief that I initially discovered was split into two categories: help for a child, and help for an adult – and much of what I read put teenagers in the adult category. The TGC is a small room of the club but, like all of its niches,[6] I found comforting similarities among us that allowed some of my grief-guilt to ease. On *Griefcast* I met other TGC members who'd also gone to a single counselling session, who felt like a giant in Lilliputland, and so never returned; or used the Dead Dad card to get out of detention; or couldn't cope at house parties any more; or talk about who fancies who; now they knew what the word 'death' really meant. Finally getting to talk to other members – despite our wildly different bereavements, roads to griefs and relationships to the dead – helped me. Finding your gang/room/fellow grief pals can show you that grief is manageable – because, somehow, other humans are living with it too.

---

[6] Niche, yes, but always worth noting that a parent of a child under eighteen dies every twenty-two minutes in the UK – around 23,600 deaths a year. This equates to around 111 children being bereaved of a parent every day. One in twenty-nine children between the ages of five and sixteen has been bereaved of a parent or sibling – that's one child in every average-sized school class. (Source: https://www.childbereavementuk.org.)

So, to my dear TGC, in case you too had trouble finding that room, here are some things I'd like to share.

The not-fun things about being a member of the TGC

1) The Ostrich

You don't really know them. Until a parent gets sick and is vulnerable, they're just sort of there, like the sofa. You don't appreciate how you might want to know actual stuff about them one day, because you're too busy trying to figure out who you are. Regrets may include: not asking them why (and how) they blew up the science lab, or what taking mushrooms and driving through London on a motorbike really felt like.[7]

2) The Magician's Trick

Many young grievers have spoken of the magician's tablecloth effect. They felt that they'd closed their eyes for a second and then someone had snatched the tablecloth out from under everything. When they opened their eyes again, it appeared as if everything was basically the same but just slightly off kilter, out of place.

It leaves you with a wobbly feeling, people dying just like that. I used to feel like I was in a swimming pool and the water was deeper than I thought it was. I kept going to put my foot down only to discover, horrifyingly, that the bottom of the pool wasn't there. One of the young grievers I spoke to on my podcast was writer and actor Brona C. Titley. When her friend Ciarra died in her early

---

[7] Probably great and highly dangerous.

twenties, Brona described it as like living in a terrarium, and suddenly the lid had been lifted off and someone had snatched a person away before slamming the lid back down again. We spoke of the shock and the fear of learning so young that death can so quickly take, ruin and destroy; that something or someone had more control over your life than you did.

3) The Freeze

Grief has the power to freeze you. After my dad's quick diagnosis and death, I was in shock. His death stopped my internal clock – as if my childhood had also died and life was now rushing past – when all I wanted to do was slow it down for a second and try and preserve the girl he knew. The reality is you can't stop time, you keep on growing and living. But that trauma can cause you to get stuck emotionally at the age you were when it happened. Later in life, when faced again with stress, it's often the place you go back to.

This is a universal truth of grief: it can feel hard to move past the age you were when they knew you. But being in the TGC means that where we stopped was in the middle of a process of transformation. Of course, I couldn't physically freeze myself – I did change, time still existed – but I cut a piece of my teenage heart and brain out and I locked them away to make sure she, the teenager who knew him, wouldn't die. And so, in a way, if the girl he knew was alive, then he hadn't quite died either. A logical madness that only grief can justify.

What was the cost of this sacrifice, of never letting go of my fifteen-year-old self? Whenever time did remind me of how much had changed, I was taken aback, I was hurt. Eventually, I realised I needed to let go of her. And him. I realised keeping her alive was suffocating me.

Great things about being in the TGC

1) The Surfer
Being in the TGC means you have a lot of time to process things, more time without them than with them. You may experience more waves of grief but, precisely because of this abundance, you get very skilled at recognising them. 'Ah, here comes another one,' you think to yourself as you stroll off to buy three massive bars of chocolate, some rum and sign into your Netflix account to watch all ten series of *Friends*. It doesn't make the waves any easier in the moment, but you learn to realise that they don't last, that they soften, that the gaps between them can get longer. That you can survive them.

2) The DDC/DMC* Card (*delete as appropriate)
I use it a lot less these days, but if you ever need to use the Dead Dad/Dead Mum/Dead Grandma/Grandpa/ Brother/Sister/Friend/Person-You-Loved card, you should. There are too few perks of this club not to use the ones it does offer. I used it most successfully (and guiltily) to avoid a detention at school. To be fair, my dad's anniversary had been the day before. We had all been caught smoking and I was about to be bollocked quite badly. So I threw it down: 'Oh, sorry Miss, it's just it was my dad's anniversary yesterday and I'm feeling a bit crap ... ' She stared at me — to this day I'm not quite sure if she knew what I was doing or not — and sent me home (while the other smokers got

detention). It felt good. It felt ... nice. To get something sort of jolly out of the shitshow. Use wisely but use guilt-free when you need to.

3) The Fire

Now, this is on a limited-time offer, but excitingly you do not have to be in the TGC to purchase. Many grievers I have spoken to have experienced 'the fire'. It's the feeling of being untouchable after a loss. The internal cautious voice that lives within most of us – should I ...? Is it okay if I ...? Will they mind if I ...? – disappears. You are liberated from caring about what anyone thinks of your actions. Actor and writer Robert Webb's mum died of breast cancer when he was seventeen. He described how, 'You couldn't really imagine something worse happening to me than my mum disappearing, so that in a sense emboldened me.'

It's hard to define how the fire will manifest; it isn't a feeling you can summarise into neat anecdotes. It's a complete change in your outlook. Whatever mattered before suddenly matters not at all. Your normal worries float away like ash on the wind. You don't care what people think or say or what you should be doing at a certain time. Nothing matters, because they are dead and so, therefore, nothing matters.

I estimate (very unscientifically) that the fire lasts about five years before it starts to dwindle and you return to being a normal person in society. But while it's aflame, it creates a heat that can drive you. After a death, this fire emboldens you, sometimes brazenly, sometimes selfishly. For me 'the fire' became a liberation: I had somehow survived this terrible thing that had almost destroyed my life. I was still alive, and I believed that nothing could hurt me any more than what had just happened. You are left with only your most necessary and essential feelings, which is a kind of freedom. And wrapped up in this new freedom is a relief – that the process is over (especially if the death is from a terminal illness). It's over. However, they died – painfully, tragically, peacefully – it's done.

JESS MILLS

For me, anyway, grief has been a very expansive experience. It hasn't felt restrictive or restraining. It's actually been incredibly expanding, to the point where I feel I've seen, it's like seeing, colours of the rainbow that you didn't know existed before. And I feel like the life-changing, really sort of reorganising experience of grief that I've been through in losing my mum, has given me windows into feelings and a comprehension of things that I didn't know existed before, and there's incredible richness in that as well.

The fire isn't universal, but I've found that a lot of young grievers have experienced a powerful surge after the death. It's a desire not to die, to be free of death. I felt that after watching my dad die. A force began to push me. I wanted to breathe. I wanted to take in huge lungsful of air, to know I was here, that I was living. Many griefsters have a sense of guilt at this urge to live; it can feel as if you're running away from the person who has died. But it's not: it's running from death itself – particularly after a hospital death, where the air is thinner, where you speak quietly, where everything about the process is designed to ease someone away from

living. Morphine, doctors, needles, curtains drawn back –
I wanted so badly to run from that. This spark, of wanting
to live, becomes a fire and it starts to burn. Now you know
the secret to life: there is no control or choice in how you
die. It will, at some point, just happen.

The fire is not always pleasant, and I've seen it manifest in
all sorts of ways. I've seen obliteration after grief, another
death in itself. I've seen recklessness: the young person
determined to live by taking advantage of every experience
going, no matter how dangerous or unsafe. At first I felt
shattered into pieces. What did my future matter? After
his death, what did anything matter? While some may find
themselves driven down a new path, I was released from
caring about what people thought – a place of freedom
I now sometimes nostalgically miss.

Malcolm Gladwell refers to his own version of 'the fire'
in his book *David and Goliath*. He calls those experiencing it
'eminent orphans' and draws on findings from several studies
showing that many successful people lost parents at a young age.
One study found that 67 per cent of British prime ministers
had lost a parent before the age of sixteen[8] – twice the rate of
parental loss for members of the British upper class, the social
group where most PMs came from.[9] The same pattern was
found among US presidents: twelve of the first forty-four US
presidents lost fathers while they were youngsters.

Initially, such patterns were dismissed as coincidences,
but as more studies found a link between young
bereavement and success, researchers began to question

---

[8] Bet Gladstone would have been annoyed to sit in a tiny chair too.
[9] The glorious British political system.

141

why early trauma might encourage you to achieve. They had found the fire that comes after grief, and a bizarre by-product of this devastation was that, sometimes, it helped the person achieve great things later.

Gladwell refers to the 'Blitz spirit' among Londoners in the Second World War, a phenomenon not predicted by the authorities. The government had been anticipating mass panic and yet, as we know, this didn't materialise. Life carried on amid unbelievable trauma. What was expected to be a point of weakness proved to be a morale (and propaganda) booster. In the months after the Blitz, Cambridge University psychiatrist and lecturer J. T. MacCurdy studied people's responses to the bombings and categorised them into three distinct groups. Firstly, those killed by the bombs weren't running through the streets creating panic – because they were dead. Next, there were the 'near misses', those near enough to the blast to experience it and see the destruction, who felt relief and shock that they'd survived. Then there were the previously uncounted 'remote misses': people living near enough to have heard the blast, felt their homes shake, but who survived physically unscathed. This calculation of fate became a heady mix for the survivors; they nearly died, and afterwards they felt strangely invincible. There are accounts of people spending one night in an Anderson shelter, surviving, and never going back to the shelter again.

Such hardiness has become mythologised in British history, but Gladwell points out that it just seems to be how people react to trauma, regardless of how Cockney they are or how stiff their upper lip is. The government had not underestimated the Great British spirit, but they

142

had assumed 'that there is only one kind of response to something terrible and traumatic. There isn't. There are two.' It can be a shock to discover that the trauma of early loss can strengthen you in a way no one expects.

Anyone who has lost a parent at a young age is aware of this. Your reaction may not always fit with what you or those around you expect. You can, shocking as it may sound, thrive after a death. That doesn't mean you're happy they're dead; that's not why you are fearless. You can thrive after death *because* of it. (The TGC are often forced to act like this is a weird coincidence to their grief but, having spoken with so many in this part of the club, I know it's not. It's an instinctive choice. Not an easy one, or always a totally conscious one; it's something more primal than that.) A parental death or a significant grief as a teenager isn't a bomb dropping on your head, but it can feel like that – like your whole world has been destroyed and now you are staring at the blast crater of where a human used to be. To have that experience is both awful and oddly exhilarating.

Where, for me, Gladwell misses some of the fullness of this experience is by placing it only in one emotion – courage. It is a bravery, but one so wrapped in sadness and pain that it hurts to wear it. So yes, I can be brave: I was strong because I had to be. This resilience comes at a great price, but I won't feel bad about the positive effects of it any more. There are enough negative ones to counteract them.

Another important point that Gladwell makes is that, like future heads of state, prisoners are also two to three times more likely to have lost a parent in childhood. The trauma of losing a parent in your formative years doesn't guarantee you a job at Number 10; having parents who can afford to send you to Eton before they die is a much safer bet. Whether you are driven to succeed or pulled under cannot be so easily boiled down to a death in the family when, of course, there are so many other socio-economic factors to be measured first. But the fact is: the fire exists – a nagging sense that for a while the death gave you something, as it took something larger.

FELIX WHITE

> When we achieved certain things in the Maccabees, I would suddenly get very sad. So, we'd be working towards something, like the last record went to number one, and I was suddenly obsessed with getting this record to number one for a couple of weeks – and it happened. When I got the call to say it was, I was suddenly overwhelmed with being really sad … The person you want to tell, you can't.

The TGC has not been an easy club to be in. I've railed against it – and I've screamed at the tide many times. But, as ever, the knowledge that I wasn't alone in this room has helped me live here. Others have felt what I have and carried on. Remind yourself constantly that whichever room of the club you're in, it's full. Full to the brim with other humans who have pieces of their hearts missing too. They are surviving after the blast. And you can too.

Wave — 2008

I don't remember when the ashes were collected or delivered, whether my mum went by herself. She must have done, I didn't go. All I know is that he was put in the wardrobe and stayed there for ten years. He was in a plastic bag, white with no logo on it. I guess cremation services don't need much branding.

There are two wardrobes in my parents' room, built into the two alcoves either side of the old fireplace. They are big and pine with Laura Ashley handles. The doors don't move well on the thick carpet, you really have to pull to drag them open. One used to be his and one hers. Eventually she commandeered both, although his suits still hung in there for years afterwards. Suits and ties and shirts — a silk scarf with ducks on it that he was very proud of; a tux; his wedding shirt with its incredible M. C. Escher bird design in orange, white and brown, with a collar you could sail on. She always joked about him being in the wardrobe and I thought little of it until, one day, I was rummaging around to 'borrow' some shoes or a bag, and there he was. The white plastic bag.

'What's this, Mum?' I shout.

'What?' she shouts back (my family don't ask, we shout into the next room/downstairs/the garden, until we're

145

heard). 'What?' she shouts again. She won't move either, a stand-off will occur until one of us shouts too loudly.

'In the wardrobe!'

'What?'

'The bag! In the wardrobe.'

'What bag?'

'The bag!'

'What bag?'

'The bag!'

'What bag? Oh, for god's sake.' She stomps upstairs and I point at it, she looks at it and without missing a beat – 'Oh, that's your dad.'

'Just there? Just in the bag?'

'Yes! What else am I supposed to do with him?'

I couldn't think really, so I took a black velvet evening bag I liked the look of and closed the door with some effort.

I can't remember when we decided it was time, but we knew it was time. It was coming up for ten years and I think we all felt a bit bad that he was still in the wardrobe. I couldn't even say he wouldn't mind, as actually I think he would have done by then.

We decided on Wales. It seemed fitting. We'll take him back to where he started. I have no idea if he was a particularly proud Welshman, another conversation we never got to have. I remember he once made us watch rugby and wore a Welsh shirt, but it didn't feel especially heartfelt. He was born outside Cardiff, a sleepy village where the Lloyds ran a sweet shop. 'We could have been the next Sainsbury's!' my grandpa used to say. But we weren't.

We'll take him back to Wales, to the land of his fathers. Alongside the industrial views are landscapes that can hold your hand and settle you. We'll go to Wales, to the sand dunes we used to play in when he took us back there. Where he camped as a kid with his brothers. (My grandpa told me the only reason these sand dunes existed was because a Hollywood film crew dumped the sand there in the 1950s. Lies. We're good at that as a family. He told me his middle name was Merlin, and that we were descended from the great Welsh magus. I believed him until, as an adult, I clocked his middle name was actually Mervyn. The fact Merlin isn't real didn't seem to register.)

We go to Wales, a drive we've made many times. But now we're a three. It's raining, of course. It's always raining when we cross the bridge. I remember my brother needing an inhaler and us finding a pharmacy in Port Talbot. 'Where you from then?' the pharmacist asked him in a thick South Walian accent.
  'London.'
  'Oh, is it big?'
  'Sorry?'
  'London, is it big?'
  'Er, yeah. Yeah, it is.'
  'Oh, that's lovely for you.'

This kept us howling for days. We still say it now. 'That's lovely for you. To be scattering your father's ashes with some mild asthma.' There's a need to laugh. A need to drag air back into our hearts, to fill the lungs. We try not to think about it too much.

We clamber up into the dunes, find somewhere just near the sea surrounded by brush and reeds. The yellow sand slipping beneath our feet, the wind blowing, rugged but in a Welsh way, not enough to blow you over but enough to make itself known. Mum gets the Tupperware box out. We're all sad but not distraught. It feels right, timely, we're in the right place. She tips him out and the Welsh wind whisks him away from us. Although not before a large chunk of him goes straight into my eye. I laugh. Because, what? Am I in a film? This is a perfect, awful joke. It stings and my eye waters horribly, a huge bit of grit is in my eye. All I can think is, 'What bit is it? ... Does it matter now?' My mum and brother look worried, I mean, this could be next-level upsetting.

Am I upset? I look at the sea and the sand, knowing he would have walked here, would have dreamt here, hoped here. I feel closer to him than I have done in many years, and I laugh. Because of course I do, he's in my eye. I laugh at the stupidity of it all. I laugh at how silly it is that people die and we are so sad about it. I laugh because it's funny and, in the midst of the well of sadness, it's nice to breathe again.

The Questions I wonder

Why did you get expelled?
How did Grandpa get you back in school?
Why did you get a motorbike?
Who taught you to drive?
What food did you like as a child?
When did you first get drunk?
Why were you in that cult for a bit?
What did it feel like, after the motorbike accident,
when they said you wouldn't walk again?
When did you think, 'Oh I'll run a marathon?'
Why were you cross?
Why did you shout?
When did you think, 'We don't get on that well?'
Did you try and change that?
Did you feel bad for working a lot?
How did you cope with us when we were small?
Did you love us?
Was it easier with a boy than me?
Do you remember reading to me?
Did you think you were a good parent?
Did you think we had turned out okay?
Were you furious to die?
What did you wish you had done?
What do you wish you had said?

I wish I had asked you.

Wave — 2010

I want to try counselling.
I want to try something.
Because it's all bubbling up in me.
The door is opening, and the cupboard is full, and the kettle is boiling over.
I need help.
I google, I shout into the internet, 'Help me.' I have no idea what I need, I'm just trying to find someone I can talk to. I know it will be about my dad, but I don't say that out loud. Grief is still lingering under the words, stressed and tired, hiding in plain sight.

I search for someone with Bereavement listed as their specialist subject. I wonder if I really want to talk to someone with Bereavement as their specialist subject.

I find someone around the corner. I feel sick walking there, I don't want to do it. I will my feet to walk forwards, which is something I have to do a lot nowadays — will my feet to walk on stage, to walk into parties, to walk into auditions, will them to keep going. Perhaps I learnt it in the aftermath of his death — just keep walking. I know how to walk forwards, I know how to do that. I can walk through things without stopping.

Her practice is her house. Why have I chosen somewhere so close?

I'll walk past this house again; I'll see her at the tube station.

It feels uncomfortable to walk into someone else's life and admit you're not okay.

It feels sordid and mental.

I don't know where to begin.

'He died? He's dead? I'm not okay. That's all, I'm not okay.'

I now have anxiety, nervousness, cyclical thinking, IBS, and constant fear, to add to my title of 'Bereaved'. I wonder if I'm suffering from being twenty-eight and if it's actually nothing to do with my dad at all. Poor bastard, always getting the blame.

I can't make this into a neat sentence, I waffle and jump from tab to tab.

She listens and I start to take notice of her. Not just notice, I fastidiously judge every inch of her. She has black, frizzy hair. Really frizzy. Look, no shade, but I have frizzy hair too, and it's not 1955. There's serums containing silicones available for us now, and we all know about them.

Her eyeliner is insane, why does this bother me so much? She's tried to do a thick, black, winged line but she's left a gap above her eyelashes. I'm supposed to be talking about death. I'm not. I'm thinking about her eyeliner. Why hasn't she checked it? She's working from home; she must walk past a mirror. How can I talk to her about the biggest topic of all, death? How can I express the human need to understand where someone goes, what happens to us all, when she can't get her bloody eyeliner straight? She's proven herself untrustworthy with this ineptitude. If you can't get something so basic correct, if your friends can't tell you it hasn't worked, your husband doesn't love you enough to say, 'Darling, it looks weird', then how can I be expected to unravel my mess in front of you?

She's still listening. I'm not.

She plays the part of therapist very well I think, head tilted just a little, sat in a cream Ikea chair, low and leant back. Her face is neutral. (Apart from the eyeliner. God, I'm ridiculous.)

Then, worse, I hear her children. I HEAR them.

I am thrown. She has a family, they live here. Do they mind? Do they think it's weird? Will they see me? I'm talking now. No idea what I'm saying. She nods, slightly.

There's a woollen rug on the floor, with tassels at either end. It makes it look like a student bedroom. I am dissecting her piece by piece – so I can pull apart her life, examine it and pay no attention to my own.

We get to him. Death. Dead. Grief. I don't normally talk about it like this. I talk in jokes and throwaway comments, and I am in control of the information.

I am terrified. As soon as I try to speak about him, I'm in floods. I can't even make words. Just tears and tears, not even sobbing, just like I've turned on a tap. I'm embarrassed and confused. Where is this coming from? It was years ago. Why am I falling apart?

A week passes. I will my feet to walk me to another session.

Then I can prove I gave it a proper try.

No one can say I didn't give it a proper go (like last time).

Afterwards, I leave her family house and therapy room numb.

It's cold and dusk is falling. The sky is turning a grey-blue. My feet feel like lead, I can barely drag them forward. But that's all I know how to do – keep moving. She's slowing me down, I decide. She's making it harder to exist. Talking is making it worse.

I have a gig that night and I'm broken. I can't scrabble myself back together. I feel like I've got no skin on, it feels like early-days grief. It's awful, uncontrollable. I can't be funny, I can't hide. I can't hide myself in a character, I'm just my sadness and it's huge. It's awful.

I begin to wonder if perhaps I'm not ready to talk about it yet.

===

From: Cariad Lloyd
Subject: Re: Appointment
To: Therapist in this interlude
Date: Wednesday, 17 October 2012, 18:34

I just found out I'm filming on the Friday and Monday so I can't see you on those days.*

Also, I think I'd like to take a break from the sessions.** You've been very helpful but I feel like I'm not quite ready to talk about some things,*** and I would like to just get some space before I come back to them.****
Thank you for the sessions, they were very useful.*****
Best wishes,

Cariad

*This bit isn't true
**true
***really true
****not true
*****true – but I don't know that yet.

155

5

A Light to Guide You

> But we call it lembas or waybread, and it is more
> strengthening than any food made by Men ... Eat a
> little at a time, and only at need. For these things are
> given to serve you when all else fails ... One will keep
> a traveller on his feet for a day of long labour, even if it
> be one of the tall Men of Minas Tirith.
>
> J. R. R. Tolkien, 'Farewell to Lórien', The Fellowship of the
> Ring (The Lord of the Rings)

I'm a *LOTR* geek – I hope that doesn't make you
immediately put this book down. I love it because it's
all about an epic journey towards an actual Mountain
of Doom, one that the characters mostly don't want to
make, but know they have to. What could better represent
grief? On their long journey, the hobbits need something
to sustain them (there's not a lot of takeaway on the path
to Mount Doom), so the elves gift them a magical biscuit
called lembas bread.[1] They only need to nibble a corner
and it will give them the strength to keep going when they
think they've nothing left.

For grief, this most arduous of quests, we need our own
version of lembas bread. When we feel like we can't go on,

---

[1] If you don't know the books, know that four furry small creatures (hobbits) have to take
a cursed ring to Mount Doom to destroy it because men are idiots and ruin everything.
Elves, dwarves and wizards help them along the way. It's incredible. The films are also
amazing: I cried when I finished the thirty-six hours of DVD extras. No, I'm not great at
endings – thanks early bereavement.

we need to reach into our packs and find something magical that can sustain us. For me, the most sustaining thing has been talking. From actual therapy to the therapy of talking to people I love – and, at its most extreme, to creating a podcast where I talk about death every week – talking has allowed me to keep going when I no longer thought I could. Maybe not as magical as lembas bread, or as tasty as a chocolate Hobnob, I grant you, but very comforting.

I believe that what griefsters need (and what society finds hard to provide) is a space where we can talk about the dead, where you can say their name, remember their good parts and their flaws equally – a space to light a candle for them with words – and where you can keep remembering them until you're 'done'. If you can gift yourself this tasty magical biscuit, it makes carrying the grief-mess easier. It helps you understand what's in your heavy luggage, lets you see what you can discard along the way back to Hobbiton.[2]

The road to finding my biscuit (yeah, I'm going to stick with this metaphor) was both long and short. Naturally I'm a talker (every school report I've ever had said I needed to stop chatting[3]) and at home I was taught that communication was not just important: it held a family together. I was trained from an early age that talking about your feelings or emotions is essential to keep a house running smoothly.[4] We would have regular family meetings.

---

[2] Hobbiton is like a lovely Teletubbyland, but without a creepy sun or mad hoover: more beer and more dancing, same amount of partying.

[3] Look at me now! Chatting is a job!

[4] I should mention that my dad worked in PR and marketing and, for most of my life, he ran his own business from home, so to him, the house really was another department in his empire.

Every Sunday we'd gather round the extendable table and discuss our goals, thoughts or dreams for the future. I once found a piece of paper from my four-year-old self with my goals written down on it (1: Practise my ballet. 2: Put shoes away). The spirit of the Lloyd after-lunch meeting wasn't pushy. For my dad, who very much led the meetings in Dad CEO mode, communication equalled connection. We'd sit munching our Sunday lunch – roast chicken or, if we were really lucky, Bernard Matthews' turkey roll[5] – and then we would talk. My family *liked* discussing things, still does; it's a pastime for us, like other families like hiking or puzzles.

And so, in the months after he died, we did as we always did, we talked. We talked about him. We said his name. I never felt any pressure to pack my grief away and move onwards. The remaining unit, my mum and my older brother, created a place open to grief, to emotions. It was always okay to cry, to feel, to bring up an ancient row or a memory – to recall his epic presence, his faux pas, his complete lack of embarrassment when he farted in front of our friends – whatever aspect of his life or death we wanted to remember or criticise. It would end in laughter, mostly, a conscious choice not to end in sadness.

Most importantly, this space was always available to me. Being a teenager meant I often couldn't describe how I was feeling, but I still had somewhere to pour that emotion. My mum (thank you Mum) endured many a loud talking (also known as shouting) session. She always stood fast, allowed

---

[5] Don't question what it is, just eat its delicious-tasting 'rind'. Don't ask why turkey has a rind. It does and it's delicious.

me to be emotional, to talk in fits and starts when I could find the words, accepted it when all I could find was rage. We would part and then come together again, often drawn back in by one of us experiencing grief in a new painful way. I saw my brother cry; I saw my mum cry. We would all cry, until the sobbing turned into laughter — 'If you don't laugh you cry,' we said over and over again. It didn't take the grief away, or the painful confusion I felt at being a grieving teenager, but I knew that if I wanted to talk, if I felt able to, they would both listen. They were there in such a profound and steady way that it didn't matter if I couldn't always talk to them. I know it gave me the strength to carry on, knowing I had a safe space to take that grief.

When *Griefcast* began, and the emails from listeners started arriving, I was astounded to hear from people who hadn't talked about their grief with close family. A listener wrote to me to say that his father had died in a tragic accident when he was a child, yet he'd never told his wife about what had happened. Others, who'd lost parents as children, had to deal with other family members making the decision that the parent wasn't to be mentioned any more. There were painful memories of not being allowed to say their name or bring up the past; of being forced to leave it behind and act like the person hadn't died, almost as if they had never existed. I received so many messages from people describing a grief experienced in silence, of a family who never celebrated a birthday or an anniversary, never allowing them to be present in this time. My guests also had stories of grief packed away to the point where the death anniversary couldn't even be recalled — it had gone unmentioned for so long it was now forgotten.

Everyone grieves differently and if you choose to grieve in silence that is, of course, a very different thing to being forced to grieve alone. Author Richard Beard wrote an incredible book, *The Day That Went Missing*, about his brother Nicky, who drowned in the sea when they were both children. Richard spoke to me about how little was discussed after Nicky's death and the effect this had on his memories.

RICHARD BEARD

I didn't know whether Nicky's body had ever been found, I didn't know the date when it happened, I didn't know the month when it happened, I didn't know where it was. I was in my mid-forties when I started thinking, 'This is ridiculous.' I knew nothing about him except for ten or eleven photos of his existence and his old cricket bat in a bucket in my mum's shed. That was about all I knew.

Eventually, even in my own family, we began to talk about it less. It felt like we had said it all. We'd hashed out the feelings and now we were left with our own grief, the mess that only we could carry. Marriage, kids – other things, louder distractions than our past pain, began to dominate the conversations. I felt like my mum and my brother had reached a peace with it all. I longed to be more forward-looking, but something kept making me look back over my shoulder. I couldn't and didn't feel at peace or 'done'. I felt in grief still, not every day but often, still pained by my memories. Hadn't I said all there was to be said? Why did I still want to talk? It felt like an itch at the back of my throat. I wasn't done. I wasn't finished talking.

In 2016, I was walking down the road thinking, 'If I had a podcast I'd probably just talk to people about death,' and I laughed to myself because it was such a terrible idea. But it dug a hole in my brain, pulled up a chair and settled in.

How would it work? Just ask people about death? Could I simply do what I had been doing – occasionally stumbling upon those in the club, finding that golden moment when another person wanted to talk about grief? We would both sigh and relax our shoulders and finally talk to someone who got it, who didn't run away; find others who understood this compulsion to speak their stories, to say their name – to say I had a dad and he's dead – and in that to feel less alone. 'If it could be that,' I thought, 'if I could just talk to people about their grief stories, maybe a few others would take comfort?'

I was pregnant as the idea began to grow. I needed to sort my life out, not make a depressing podcast. No, I told myself, it wouldn't work. I put the idea down, walked away from it. But, like the baby inside me, it grew and kicked and punched my insides until I couldn't ignore it. So I gave in. Fine, I thought, I'll record some chats ... I'll record them, stick them somewhere and do no more – because I'm having a baby, not a podcast.

Griefcast was born. I discovered that, yes, it was just like having those chats I'd been stumbling upon since I was fifteen, but the microphone made it permanent. Finally, nothing was lost to the ether when I spoke to someone else in the club. I could ask more. I could be really curious – but how did you survive that? How did you cope? And the guests wanted to talk, they wanted to cry and remember, they longed to talk, just as I did.

From the very first episode, I made sure to ask my guests their person's name and to say it out loud. I wanted them to be there with us. I didn't want it to be just sadness and grief. I wanted it to reflect my own experiences: a mess — a sad, happy, painful, stupid, funny mess that swung from tears to laughter whenever it felt like it. I wanted us to talk honestly about some good things that had happened. We weren't happy they had died, but — here is the truth of how it is to grieve — what surprised us all was the after-effect of talking. The guests didn't feel sad or depressed, as you might expect from an hour's reminiscing; they felt lighter and calmer at being allowed the time to tell their story. For an hour they had been able to talk about that person without shame or embarrassment or fear about bringing death into the room. Death was welcomed in and given tea and cake. We laughed more than anyone thought we would. We found common stories and shared pain. It was of course different every time — each person's grief-mess was their own — but it felt nice to look at each other and acknowledge the swirl of tangled emotions resting and wiggling in both our hands.

I was just having a chat, that's the lie I told myself. It wasn't really about me. Yet I talked. A lot. About my dad and my grief and my pain — and an unexpected consequence of all this talking, the weekly session of grief-sifting, was that it started to help me. My tightly wound grief-mess started to unravel. Sneakily. Week-in, week-out, I was talking about my dad, and it was helping, and I felt I was healing myself as I spoke. After so many years, he was no longer the difficult dead-dad-bomb I was never quite sure I should explode. He was someone I felt at ease discussing. I found myself talking about him without my cheeks burning and my throat closing. I felt relief. It wasn't always easy. Some weeks I'd hold back my tears, dig my nails into my palms and think, 'Please get me away from this grief, I don't want it. Let me run back to the life where I just ignore it.' But I knew I couldn't go back. This wasn't really a choice any more. This was something I needed to do.

And every week we'd talk, and my guest would say something that broadened my view of the club. I spoke to people about griefs I'd never even thought of. I saw how limited my understanding of it really was. I wasn't Queen Grief at all, I was just a passing peasant in her land. As the podcast grew, we talked about different griefs – baby loss, miscarriage, suicide, losing a friend, losing a sibling, losing a stepmum; grandparents who felt like parents, parents who'd let you down, the cruelness of dementia, the suddenness of heart attacks; how different cancers take away different aspects of the person. I spoke to people in the death industry, from death doulas and death service professionals to palliative care doctors. I spoke to an array of different voices about this strange, weird process of death and grief. I felt the joy of recognition. It was nice – blissful even. I felt as if I was finally at a party I wanted to be at, the one full of people grieving, and I could easily talk about what was bubbling inside of me. I spoke to people whose grief frightened me, whose grief was so painful and so sad that I didn't know how to help. So I stopped trying to find common ground and just listened. I realised that listening to these stories was helping me; that's why I kept doing it – I felt less alone. I began to see it was a VERY large club, overwhelmingly huge. We were all here, and we were all managing it, somehow.

And then there were the emails, from all over the world, from all ages, from all different types of grief. It wasn't just me or the guests who felt better, the podcast was helping listeners too. They were relieved to know others had had similar journeys; they felt comforted, just as I did. There were short, kind messages as well as much longer letters, dense with detail. They would often end: 'You don't need to reply, it just helped me to write this down.' And I understood. A woman emailed to say she'd fallen out with her mum. Her stepdad had died, and she hadn't understood her mother's grief. She had thought her mum was wallowing in sadness; she hadn't understood what grief did to people, but she'd listened and emailed her mother and they were talking again now. Another person emailed to say her sister had died and, since then, she'd thought she was having a breakdown. But then she listened to the podcast and realised it wasn't a breakdown, there wasn't anything wrong with her; it was just grief. She wasn't okay but she would be. Another listener emailed to say they'd begun listening before their father's death. It had been hard, but hearing all of us in the club already had helped prepare them. It couldn't take away the pain, but they knew they wouldn't be alone with it; they felt the power connection can offer. There were so many messages about the pain of not talking. I still get them. I still read them.

I wasn't alone any more, I never had been. I wasn't odd for having had a parent die from pancreatic cancer at fifteen. A young woman in New Zealand wrote to me to say our lives had been almost identical. Her dad also died of the same disease when she was the same age at the same time as my dad. Even my circumstances were no longer isolating. I could see that death was always with us, always had been. We were talking about it, letting other people hear those thoughts and feelings, and I felt useful. Gloriously, wonderfully useful.

It helps to hear other people, helps us to connect with each other. When we find those crossover moments, we are no longer isolated, we are no longer alone, we are not the only person this has happened too. What happened to us isn't weird or unfair, it's human. Grief is human. Grief is the price you pay for life.

*

At the same time as starting *Griefcast*, I began therapy. Finally, I felt brave enough to not simply talk about my grief but to investigate it, guided by a professional. Therapy isn't for everyone, but it changed me, helped me and, if I'm honest, I think it saved me.[6] I couldn't hide in the therapist's room. I couldn't switch the questions back on the guest, I couldn't make stupid jokes. Each week we would open the box and out would pour all the grief. Everywhere. A huge hideous mess of it all over the place.

At first, I was shocked there was even a box that full. How was it still here, this pain? I had sealed it so tightly

---

[6] It is also a privilege, one I was lucky to get through our glorious NHS because I am educated, white and entitled enough to navigate what is (thanks to mass underfunding of essential mental health services) a tough and dismissive system. I am grateful my privilege allowed me that help and I'm aware it is not as equally available as it should be.

I assumed it would have just shrivelled up and died. It had waited, as grief does. I cried and cried and cried to admit that, yes, I was still sad about a lot of things. I was able to admit this because of talking to my podcast guests, talking to others who still felt sad, still cried from time to time. Twenty years on, thirty years on, far ahead of me in the journey, wherever they were, they normalised it – and I could allow myself to feel this way too. When I spoke to those 'fresh' to the club, when I saw their pain and rawness, I'd remember mine. I would see them try to brush the sadness away, make it disappear with an endless refrain of, 'I'm fine now, of course.' I would see them try this same trick unsuccessfully and I try to pass on advice as a Grief Elder in this frankly bleak village: that there was no point rushing through it, no point trying to hide from it. For here I was, twenty years on and still in pieces each week.

There were plants in my therapist's room. A maiden fern appeared one week. I had a maiden fern at home and, despite being excellent at keeping plants alive, it died. Maiden ferns are bloody fussy. But my therapist persisted with hers, moving it around the room, to the windowsill, to the shelf, to more shade, more light. I never commented, but each week I saw the delicate little fern wobbling and surviving, despite its fussiness. It was almost too easy to apply the metaphor to myself.

My biggest fear about therapy, the reason I had avoided it for so long, was what would happen once I started talking to someone whose questions I was afraid to answer? Once we opened that box, what then? You can't just release a bear into the room and pretend nothing has changed. It felt dangerous. I was frightened of myself, of my grief. But each week, interviewing a new guest on the show let a little air out of the box. I would feel safer having talked to my guest, safer knowing I wasn't alone, and this in turn helped the therapy – until eventually we opened it fully, and I cried and bawled and snotted, as viscerally as I had on that beach in Brighton when I thought my lungs would burst from crying. My heart and eyes ached. I raged to realise it was still so painful. I was furious it hadn't got better. But I hadn't tended it, I'd ignored it, figuring it would give up and go away. It hadn't.

So here in the therapy room I felt it and, thankfully, this time I wasn't alone. My therapist helped me through. Once I spilled it out and it was all over the floor, we could look at it clearly, with curiosity and kindness. 'Ahhhh, what is that bit? ... He didn't speak to me properly when he was dying. Perhaps that was hard for him. Perhaps you were too young and that's terribly, terribly sad. But true. That's what that bit of the mess is ...'

We talked and we unravelled the wool and wound it back again into a ball. Afterwards I would breathe so deeply, I would feel some of the grief lifting, changing, not exactly disappearing, but fading a little. And that would hurt too, to lose some of the things I'd been carrying for so long, to have to let them go as well. Loss. So much loss. Of him, of memories, of myself, of things I thought I knew. I let go of all the things fifteen-year-old, grief-filled me had nailed down as fact. I began to see them as how things were then, not how things were now. Not universal truths but truths made to survive a situation which was awful and sad and rubbish.

Then as the weeks of talking turned into years, I would leave the room, I would feel — okay. Truly okay. Not great, not awful, sort of numb and sort of fine and sort of sad. But I could carry on. I realised I was moving through the pain, I was working on it — and learning how that really did mean *work*. It proved to me I could stop and start. I could grieve and then put it down. For years I'd been convinced that if I started to open that box, started to answer those questions, I'd never stop hurting. It would become uncontrollable; my tears would drown me. The fear and terror had destroyed any sense of hope that I could do it, that I could sort through it all. I didn't believe I could. It took a long journey, many attempts and the right therapist, but now I could see it was possible. To open the box ... and then close it again. Till next week. To talk to the guests, talk to the listeners, talk to my therapist, and explore my grief, listen to others, and learn. What a strange, wonderful and complex process grief is.

No one had ever shamed me for my grief. I never felt any door had been slammed. So why had it been so hard for chatty ol' me to talk about some of the most painful memories? The answer lay with my dad, of course. I had been brought up by a talker, and yet, when he got sick, he wouldn't talk. He wouldn't discuss it. This man, this behemoth who didn't stop cycling, running, working, eating, was always on the move, was the same one dying.

Did he know he was dying? He didn't seem to believe it was possible, and so neither did I. Even as we sat on the cancer ward in hospital during those last few days, with people dying around him, he hadn't wanted to allude to death. It was deafening and confusing. One day my mum begged him to talk about funeral plans. What did he want? What should they do? 'Pete,' she said, over and over again, 'Please.'

He turned to me, his ever-present child PA, and asked me to start writing down his plans. 'Get a pen,' he said. 'We'll go to Boston for that conference and then to Findhorn[7] after that —' He looked at me with the usual mix of confusion and annoyance that I wasn't doing what he'd asked me to do. I remember rubbing my hands, wishing an adult would deal with the situation because I didn't know how to. It was his job to be a parent, why couldn't he be the sensible one here?

When I finally brought up this moment in therapy, I was voicing one of my deepest and darkest memories of his illness. 'How sick was he when you tried to talk to him?' my therapist asked me. Had I thought about how he felt in that moment? 'How much medication was he on?'

With a sad heart, I realised that I hadn't. The memory had become so painful I couldn't move past it. My grief had been wrapped up in my teenage ego and pain. For years I'd been so angry with him for his silence, for how he had never spoken to me about his impending death. My therapist helped me to stop blaming him for his silence. Her questions forced me to think as the adult Cariad, not the teenager. I can't imagine how frightening it must have been for him, at forty-four, a husband, a breadwinner for that family, a father to two children, a son, a brother. Up until he got sick, he had been extraordinarily fit and healthy, a man who ran marathons, who did triathlons, who was training for an Ironman. To suddenly be unable to walk, to suddenly be vomiting constantly. How scary the speed of it must have been for him — as much as it

---

[7] An alternative-living community in Scotland.

was for us to witness. His silence had stayed with me for a long time – that he, the adult, didn't start the conversation for me. As an adult now, I can see perhaps he just couldn't. It gave me an insight into how painful a silence can be. How much is filled with your own logic and poisonous thoughts when the truth isn't discussed. I wish he'd talked then, but maybe it wasn't possible. I still wish we'd managed to talk about it somehow. I wish I'd learnt how to talk when it was hard and not easy.

I was staggered at how painful it still was for me, all these years later (never let anyone tell you that time will dictate your emotion, it won't). I wept about how we hadn't said a goodbye, about how he hadn't given me any parting wisdom, how he'd left in the middle of a conversation. How death wasn't clean and careful and white sheets and flowers in vases. How it was messy and confusing and shitty sheets and unbearable human pain.

It had taken twenty years to blast the doors off and look inside, to see the mess that I had shoved in there and walked away from. The emotions I'd felt were so terrifying I hadn't believed I could look at them again and survive. But I did, I looked, and the bear didn't eat me, the grief didn't swallow me whole. I cried and I did not drown. I had to talk to someone else to be brave enough to know that. It's not a painless process. I'll be honest, it really hurts to open the box and see your past self sat in there, still hurting – but it was the only way I could help some of those agonising losses. To admit they were still there, to cry at what I found, and then accept that I didn't need them any more. To soften their sharpness, allow them to fade a little. I assumed grief was stagnant, but therapy showed me another path.

It wasn't until I had talking therapy that I learnt how much your grief can change. My family had been (and still are) amazing; our talks carried me through the bomb-blast first years of grief. But to sort out the deep pain I needed therapy, a safe space where I could be vulnerable and guided, and it was life-changing.

KAYO CHINGONYI
Poet. Kayo's parents both died from HIV-related illnesses when Kayo was young.

I feel like a therapist helps you find the black box recorder – 'cos you lose entirely the sense of the particular moment that was so difficult. The thing about lots of traumas is that your body protects you from them – it finds a way to protect you in the moment or afterwards – whether you dissociate or whatever protection your body presents. And I think with someone physically not being there any more, the protection is really flimsy because you're always being met with this alternate reality.

CHARLIE RUSSELL
Actor. Charlie's mum died on her eighteenth birthday from complications due to bipolar disorder and alcohol abuse.

I needed to go because I wasn't sleeping. I told myself: 'I'm not sleeping, I should go to counselling, it's not about the mum stuff.' Then it all came out. I think everyone should go [to therapy] whether they've got this big thing in their life or not, because it's sort of like going to the gym but for your mental health ... I was so angry at everyone else for not handling it. 'Why am

I so upset and nervous all the time? And I can't sleep, oh I'm crazy, I'm broken.' Actually, going to counselling made me realise there are reasons for this behaviour, it doesn't mean you're broken.

I noticed I was talking less about him on my podcast. He'd still come up of course, but I started not to need to talk about *my* grief-mess quite so much. I'd talked about him until I didn't need to any more. That's all a griefster wants: to talk about them, till they're 'done'. Is that the fear from everyone else, they can smell it – that we want to talk and we don't know when it will end? I don't have a grave to visit, or a church that I feel at home in. This was my church – of talking, of allowing myself to remember. I felt it in my guests too: to be allowed to say their person's name for an hour, to rejoice in their aliveness once more in a world that only wants the narrative to be, 'They are dead, that's The End.' It was a magical thing, to just talk about them. We conjured them up and we visited them.[8]

---

[8] This is referred to as 'continuing bonds', a theory first put forward by Dennis Klass, Phyllis R. Silverman and Steven L. Nickman (eds) in *Continuing Bonds: New Understandings of Grief* (Routledge, 1996). In this model they depart from the old-fashioned approach of 'moving on' from grief. Instead, as many people do naturally, the griever is encouraged to stay in contact with their dead loved one – through conversations, objects, dreams, altars, photos, talking – any way of keeping the dead present. There are many cultures around the world that celebrate the remembering of the dead, including some that dig up their bodies and have meals with the corpses, the Day of the Dead festival in Mexico, and the Shinto and Buddhist tradition of leaving offerings to the dead in a home altar. Just because they're dead doesn't mean you stop thinking about them, their opinions on things, what they would have thought of what you are doing. It's okay to wonder this, to have it in your head, and to know the answer. I've never met a griever who doesn't want to tell you about them: how funny they were, what food they ate, the silly things they said. All this precious information is lost if we do not give ourselves permission to talk about them.

Therapy helped me so radically that I, like a convert to a new religion, can be zealous about it. I even once asked the great Julia Samuel (or Saint Julia, as we call her on the podcast – grief psychotherapist and author of the extraordinary *Grief Works*) how I could convince people who didn't want therapy to have it. She gave me a firm look and told me that some people don't need it, that it isn't for everyone. I took what she said seriously (she's a saint, you don't muck around with them). It made me realise that my road-to-Damascus moment was just that – mine. Like my grief, it was a unique experience. If the idea of talking to someone professionally makes you want to vomit, don't worry. There are so many other ways to connect to your grief – from blogging to journaling, reading self-help books or listening to podcasts; or, the most ancient way of all, just having a cup of tea with someone who cares enough to listen and say their name with you. What matters is the connection, and the recognition that we may need a space for untangling the grief.

Eventually my grief changed into something I never ever thought was possible: it became more peaceful, something that was part of me, not something screaming to be heard. I finally understood how some of my guests had felt when they'd said they didn't cry any more. A manageable grief had seemed alien to me. But having done the talking I needed, I understood what a calm grief felt like. I was still carrying my grief-mess, it walked behind me like a scrappy dog – with me, present, but not uncontrollable. I didn't feel ashamed, I didn't fight it any more.

I carried on with *Griefcast*, and with therapy – and I finally saw past the grief to other truths, to things I had ignored, memories I hadn't unpicked because I was afraid to look at them properly. I learnt some uncomfortable things about him, I grieved a little more, but it didn't overwhelm me. It all helped. I felt like I'd been looking at the centre of a bomb blast for so long, it didn't occur to me to look past it. I'd just been staring at the event itself, the grief, the death, the pain. Once I let those things be free, once I stopped holding on to them to keep them safe, I could finally see the whole picture: of him, of my past self, of my grief. I could walk towards the future understanding where I'd come from.

Guests would email me after recording the show to say talking had stirred memories, that they'd suddenly remembered other details. For the hour that we chatted their person was with us, alive in narrative, alive in the room. I understood. I hadn't been able to finish the conversation with him in real life – but I had finished something with these chats. The talking had done something miraculous. It isn't for everyone, it isn't the only answer – but finding and demanding a space for your grief – in whatever way that manifests, can help. If we lived in a society that was less afraid, was less worried we'd never stop, perhaps we could all talk until we're done. Maybe it's naive, but maybe that's all the griefster is looking for.

Take the lembas bread, nibble it when you need to. Frodo couldn't have got to Mount Doom without it, and you have more than just men's greed and a giant spider to get past. Grief can't simply be defeated and forgotten.[9]

---

[9] Obviously, Frodo never forgot; neither did Sam nor Pippin nor Merry. #Fellowship4eva.

Magical biscuits may be hard to find for us, but there are human equivalents that exist and will help, when you're ready. Talk until you're done. Until you feel you've said what you need to say. Until you can accept that the person who was alive is now dead. Until 'dead' means something to you that makes sense. Talk to yourself, to a notebook, to a friend, to a therapist, to a counsellor, to the wall, to a voice recorder, to an audience, with psychotherapy, EMDR, CBT, journaling. You are allowed to speak it out loud. They died. You're still here and may talking keep them with you a little longer.

All Yellow

Slowly, I can remember him not sick.

It arrives one day in my head. Until now he has been yellow in all my memories. His liver went first, that's how they discovered the cancer in his pancreas. Because they were looking at his liver. It's quite common with pancreatic cancer to find something else first. It's sneaky, not many symptoms, so by the time you've found it, it's too late, like an old franc note stuck down the back of the sofa – you've missed your chance.

His eyes went yellow. Such a happy colour – sunshine, sunflowers, sunrises – but here it was like turmeric, it stained him. Dissolved all over him like the cancer. He's in hospital for his liver. Then more tests and then it's chemo for his pancreas. It's confusing. I don't know what a pancreas does.

Now, after time, I think it's a form of PTSD. All my memories of him would flash up and he'd be dying, sick, yellow, hollow. The yellowness rooted itself onto the projector in my brain, like sun exposure on my eyes, playing over and over daily: blink it was there, breathe it was there, sleep it was there. Sick, yellow, sick, sick sick.

Dying dying dying dying in front of me.

Just eight weeks of memories obliterating all that came before.

My reality blurred. Twisted reshaped around his sickness and his death.

I eventually accepted it. This life, where all he was was a dead dad, a sick dad, a dying dad, a space where he was no longer visible.

Then it just faded. Then the past came back. Other memories came back. From before yellow.

There's who we were. There he is, chasing me, being a horsy, reading to me, endless reading. The stubborn insistence I look up a word when I didn't know it. Get the dictionary down, learn to find the first three letters, search the words, find it. Now you have a new word. The frustration for us both that I could never remember what melancholy meant. It threw me, the melon bit. How can a word with melon in it mean sad? Melon! It's so nice.

The sickness became a page in the story, not the entire script. It took years, it took years to see the beginning again. That someone so loud and smelly and noisy and so LOUD was dead. Wasn't here, wasn't rustling his tracksuit bottoms down the hall, wasn't hobbling up the stairs, quick but offbeat in his rhythm; wasn't saying, 'You've got the brain the size of a planet,' if you got something right or remembered something you'd looked up; wasn't crouched over a curry of a million dishes, munching, chewing, dropping rice everywhere.

Wasn't here. But had been. Had been here.

Wave – Spring, 2012

We're getting married in May. I wanted a spring wedding; I want spring flowers.

June isn't spring in my opinion, and I have to avoid April – April is death month and so it must be May. That means I have to pass the death anniversary to get to the wedding.

I have to round the corner and get past the big GO before heading to my new life.

I thought it'd be easy; I've been prepping for years. When your dad dies at fifteen you are very aware he's not going to be at your wedding. I've had years to prepare for this. And yet it hasn't helped. I don't feel ready.

I see the date in the calendar, I feel stunned as I see the D day is marching towards me.

Weddings are stressful anyway, but this is a wedding that's saturated in grief. I've spilled it everywhere, and like ink, it's ruining my vintage white dress.

I keep arguing and snapping.

I am sitting on the bed in our tiny, rented flat arguing with my soon-to-be husband and I don't know why I'm picking at everything. The landlady's thin and faded floral curtains let in a soft glow of light. I'm crying. My body is worried, my bones, my teeth, my eyes, my nerves, my tongue, my feet, are worried. I am anxiety in a skin suit.

I feel small and ashamed. My grief is still deeply raw and painful. It's still fresh, even at twenty-nine, so far away from fifteen. It shouldn't be this deep, should it? Shouldn't I be over it?

I realise I don't want to get married because it's too grown up. It's the act of an adult, a sane rational adult who has her own plates and pays for a TV licence. It's not what fifteen-year-olds do. How can I be that person? If I'm a grown-up, then he's dead. And he is dead, isn't he?

Isn't it silly? I'm not stupid – I'd actively describe myself as clever. I understand politics and Chekhov and I can pretend to speak French. But I have convinced myself somewhere in the back of my brain, deep, deep in the basement, that he's not dead. I know he's *dead*, but not **dead** you know, actually, definitely **dead**. He's just *dead*, you know?

My memories feel scorched, branded into my head. The moment he died there was an explosion, a bang so loud it left my ears ringing. The girl who lived that is real, she's so alive, everything she felt still feels palpable. I can taste 1998. It was real. I am still staring at my parents on the sofa trying to talk to me, still stuffing my mouth so they won't hear me cry, still grasping at straws as to where my life went. I preserved it, poured jam sugar all over it and sealed it in a jar.

Now this bastard time. Bastard, bastard time. Marching on. Laughing at me.

But here I am now, 2012, not fifteen. Getting married, turning thirty, doing the things I want to do, and now more than ever I miss him, because again, fucking again, I am growing.

Away. Away. Away.

Every landmark of happiness, every big brave step forward, every time I feel joy, it fucking hurts. Because he's not there, he didn't know, and he never can. That's shit. That's painful.

My brother walks me down the aisle. I am getting married at a registry office, so, really, he just walks through a door with me. We're waiting to go in and the registrar pops his head round and says, 'All ready?!' – but he says it weirdly, in an odd tone.

Without looking at my brother I know we've both noticed it. We start laughing, giggling hysterically. My friend waiting for us inside hears our noises and is worried we are sobbing, standing there dadless. But we aren't, we are crying with laughter at the way a man pronounced 'all ready'.

Sometimes it's okay, sometimes it's funny. Sometimes on the day they're not there and they are. **Dead** and not *dead*.

I'm here. I walk forwards. I am okay. I am in pieces. I am okay and I'm here.

6

What to say

And What Not to Say

'So, where do your parents live?'

Um ... Your heart pauses for a second. WHY DO PEOPLE NEED TO KNOW THIS? You clench your drink, the icy condensation making it slip in your hands. You take a breath in ... Oh, they're still looking at you – you haven't said anything yet.

So ... yeah ... Should you go into it? Where are you? MY PARENTS? I WISH FATE HAD BEEN SO KIND. Too much. Should you lie? How bad is today? Can you speak the truth without your voice cracking? Are they in the club? Would they notice if you ran away now?

Yeah, so ... It's been too long. Just say something. Just start with the truth.
Options:

A) Say, 'My mum lives in London,' saying the 'm' in mum very firmly, in a way that makes it clear, 'DON'T ask about the dad in this situation.'

B) Say, 'My mum lives in London,' saying the 'm' in mum firmly, in a way that implies, 'Hmm, it's complicated but not traumatic' – which is a lie, but might make things smoother.

C) Say, 'My mum lives in London, but my FATHER IS DEAD.' Go all out, scream it in their faces and hope the force of your emotional outburst shuts down any further questions.

Congratulations, you chose A.

'Er, yeah. My mum lives in London.'
'And your dad?'*

(*ALERT: You are in _that_ conversation, this is not a drill, you've used your slightly hard-edged 'm' on the word mum, but it has not registered. REPEAT: it has not registered. There's nowhere left to go now.)

'Oh, um, he's – yeah, he's dead. He died when I was fifteen.'

'Oh, right. Oh, sorry. Erm, I didn't know.'
A W K W A R D P A U S E
'Ha, that's okay it's not your fault.'
'Ha! No! It isn't!'
'You didn't kill him!'
A W K W A R D P A U S E
'Ha ha, no. Well, thanks Cariad, but I have to go away from you now. You've reminded me of my own mortality and I don't like it.'

Scene

CARIAD exits the bar feeling a little more griefy than she did earlier, and weirdly guilty about upsetting someone for bringing up her dead dad, who she didn't actually bring up.

Curtain.

*

What does your **dad** do?
Where does your **mum** live?

How many **children** do you have?
How **many** brothers have you got?
How old is your sister **now**?

Questions. The questions we all innocently ask each other because, like dogs sniffing bums, we like to get a sense of who someone is when we meet them. Grievers enter a world of trying to negotiate how to tell people that your someone is ... dead actually.

You don't have to be in the club to know that we aren't great at talking about death. The mere mention of the word makes shoulders tense, stomachs gurgle and palms sweat. I have seen people tie themselves in physical knots to avoid anything grief-related coming up in light conversation. The social awkwardness we feel when talking about death comes, unsurprisingly, from a place of fear. That might be a fear of upsetting a griever, fear of not saying the 'right' thing or making their day worse than it already is. So. Much. Anxiety. And this leads to people either avoiding the conversation, changing the subject, saying nothing at all (so weird), or making the sort of blundering, ill-thought-through comments that a griefster has to get adept at handling (especially in the first year, when it feels like you have to explain that they're dead on a tortuous, almost daily, basis). We will all die; we all know someone who has died – shouldn't we have got really good at talking about it by now?

My dear griefsters, I want us to exhale and relax. Here is a safe space where we can admit how upsetting, annoying and infuriating some of the things people say to us are.

We've all experienced it – the thoughtless comment, the insensitive question. We've all gone back to another griefster to laugh/cry our heads off at what some people think is acceptable death chat.

After my dad died, my mum received an official letter addressed to him. But rather than retyping out who it was addressed to, they'd simply crossed out my dad's name and written 'DEAD' next to it, and then sent it to my mum. Incredible. Another time, someone said to me, after I first mentioned to her my dad was dead, that if *her* dad was dead she'd tell everyone because she was sure you'd get 'so much attention' because of it. Reader, I stayed silent and changed the subject, as I had no idea how to unpick that one.

We all have stories of the mad and hurtful things that have been said to us over the years. Funny occasionally, but often they sting. I'm so sorry we have these added wounds to tend to on top of the grief.

ADAM BUXTON

Comedian, writer, podcaster. Adam's father died at home after he had been caring for him for some months.

There was one guy who came round – he was not a Macmillan guy; he was from another caring agency – he came pretty close to the end. And one of the worst things was when my dad couldn't really move or get out of bed, but he still needed to go to the toilet and stuff. So there'd be a complicated procedure; I won't go into too much detail, but this guy was helping me with it. My dad would be moaning and groaning, and I was obviously finding it very stressful and upsetting – and this guy looks over and says,

'Hang on a second, I know you! ...' – which is the worst one, in real life anyway, when someone dimly thinks they know you and you don't want to say, 'Oh well, I'm on TV, I'm famous!' because probably that's not how they know you. Maybe you've bought a pint off them, or they know you from some other way, so you don't want to presume, 'Oh you've seen me on TV,' especially at that moment.

I was like, 'I don't think you do.'

He said, 'Well you look very, very familiar though.'

Well, I don't know: do you watch *8 Out of 10 Cats Does Countdown*? I'm on that sometimes. Dictionary Corner? Ring any bells? ...

To the non-club members, hello, hi – *waves in a friendly font** – thank you for being here. I know it's hard to walk into somewhere where you don't understand the rules, it can feel uncomfortable and awkward.[1] This isn't a blame game. In the long run, we can better help those grieving if we all admit that this is a heavy and awkwardly shaped rock that we're trying to push up the hill (behind a hearse). Most of us have little practice talking about death, there's no GCSE in grief management.[2]

Grief is strange and complex. If I struggle to understand my own grief, then of course others will struggle to find the right thing to say to me. I'm still not perfect at talking about it; no one is. And I know this can make it seem futile to attempt saying anything at all.

---

[1] I went to a music festival once.
[2] THERE SHOULD BE.

Hold that thought though, because, truthfully, the mistake so many of us make is in trying to find the right thing to say, searching for ways of making it better. There will always be the blunt, short exchanges with strangers. These, sadly, are just a part of life with grief – having to explain they're dead, you live in a flat, you've got a brother – whatever piece of information they need to know about you. To the ones who want to help, who are searching for the words, how do we help when words fail us? What if you can't make it better but you can still be there? What if there is always going to be a wrong thing to say because everyone's grief is different? What if we start with, 'I don't know what to say but I want you to know I'm here ...'?

I have got better at dealing with people's panic in the moments when I have to say, 'He's dead actually.' I can now remain calm. Telling someone that my dad is dead doesn't frighten me (as much) any more. With time I've learnt to judge the moment. I can check in with myself first: am I okay? How vulnerable do I feel? If it's a good day, I'll be honest. And if it's not, I've learnt how to set boundaries.

That has taken time. The early days were different. As a rageful teenager I got a crass sense of satisfaction from bringing it up – because the person I was talking to (telemarketing caller in 1998) then felt bad and, at that point, so did I, so it felt fair. 'Is Mr Lloyd there?' was greeted with a cheerful, 'No, because he's dead!' It felt weirdly powerful to be able to deliver the news to someone who wasn't prepared for it. (Yes, I think I was playing out what had happened to me to gain control over it. See, therapy does work.) There would be a pause and a hasty, 'Oh, I'm so sorry –', met by a counterattack from me (I was ready), 'Are you?'

The key here was to really draw out the moment. If you kept silent you could let that sentence hang thick in the air, a giant helium balloon of awkward awfulness. 'There you go cold-caller, my life has gone to shit, congratulations, you're now in it too.' The gleeful, mischievous feeling would dissipate quickly, though. They would put the phone down and I would be back watching telly and realising my dad was still dead. A brief bubble of control in a bath of despair.

It wasn't until many years later that I experienced being on the other side of the grief river. After my husband's mum died, when we were in our thirties, I was suddenly faced with being the person who said the wrong things, who didn't understand, who couldn't make it better. This was new to me. I had spent so much of my life being in grief, being the one annoyed at other people's stupid comments, rolling my eyes at their attempts to deal with my grief, thinking it was their fault, that they should know better – that I didn't know any better. With my mother-in-law's death I learnt that it isn't any easier on the opposite bank. Yes, less painful – I wasn't in grief's harsh glare. But I was watching someone I loved in pain, and it was awful. I was consistently getting it wrong despite knowing him best, despite being experienced with grief. Of course, part of my frustration was that I, Grandma Grief, didn't know how to make it better. I was trying to fix his grief because then it would ... be done. I wanted to take the pain from him, but I couldn't. (*Foolish Cariad. You can never take the pain of grief from someone; they need it. That's what's left – the pain that their person is gone. To take it would be to act like that person had never existed: the pain is proof that they lived.*)

192

One day I realised that everything I was doing to 'help' my husband wasn't working. He didn't want to talk about it, or shout about it. He was dealing with grief very differently to me. Of course he was. He wasn't a teenager, his relationship with his dead parent was different to mine. Why was I trying to make him dance to my death tune? When I acknowledged this, I could finally see what he needed. I saw that there wasn't a right way to do this, there were a million different ways. He didn't need me to bring my grief into it, or fix it, or make him feel better; he just needed to be heard. He didn't need to scream about it, or chat; he simply needed someone to sit quietly with him. Each grief is personal, unique. We can all appreciate the terrible pain of grief, but we need to listen meticulously to truly understand what someone needs.

The only way I learnt how different all griefs were was by talking to people. These are not always easy conversations to have, but every time we do allow death to be discussed, if we listen, and don't seek a magic phrase that will make it all better – but truly listen to what someone has been through – we will learn. When it's a grief that terrifies you or triggers you personally, it's important to admit it's a scary thing to do. So start from a place of acceptance: 'This is difficult for me to talk about.' That doesn't mean you can't help or won't help. We need to begin from a place of honesty, so that we *can* help.

After starting *Griefcast* I came to realise that there were certain griefs that frightened me. I could talk about dead parents until the zombies rose up and took over. But children dying? That was terrifying. Suddenly I had nothing to say at all. As the podcast gained momentum, listeners would contact me requesting specific griefs to be covered. I agreed: I wanted the podcast to reflect as many experiences as possible. But I was afraid to have some of those conversations. Just like the people I'd rolled my eyes at for years, here I was desperate not to talk about death, because I was scared.

Speaking to writer Jayson Greene was one of the hardest conversations about grief I've ever had. In 2015 his daughter, Greta, was killed in a tragic accident in New York when she was just two years old. She was sitting with her grandmother on a bench when a piece of masonry fell off a building and landed on her. Even writing it down now, I feel shocked by the truly hideous nature of what his family suffered. It terrified me, this grief. Everything in my bones, my tissues, my muscles told me not to talk to him. Discussing this death felt dangerous – that even talking about it was somehow dangerous to my children, as if it was catching – a completely unjust and irrational feeling, but a reminder that the urge to run away from death is pretty universal. It's not as simple as rudeness or cruelty; it's self-protection. When someone tries to squirm away from your grief, it may help to remember that there is some primal drive in them – to hide/fight/flee – fearing that death will come for them next.

I booked the interview and met up with Jayson, despite my pounding heart. I breathed slowly and I thought of all the times people had acted like Dead Dad was contagious and how stupid (and upsetting) that had been. I knew I needed to hear Jayson's story. I knew someone out there might be helped by hearing it on the podcast. Jayson had written an incredible book about his experiences (*Once More We Saw Stars*); he had been brave and fearless enough to share his story. The least I could do was listen to him.

Once your own fear isn't demanding your attention, then you can hear what someone's story really is. We have a duty as humans to not turn away from each other. Walk with them. Listen to what happened. Just be there.

JAYSON GREENE
Author and journalist. He describes here how he and his wife were supported by friends and family after the accident.

They knew that we needed to be held and they did, they held us up. I mean we had this incredible community of people who brought food every day of the week, who just sat with us, who talked about silly things with us because they knew we needed to pass the time, who treated us in some ways like it was just another day, but who understood that it wasn't and there were so many ways in which we were just cared for. Even if someone said something somewhat clumsy in the grand scheme, it never mattered to me; we're not talking about etiquette, this is not the realm of those things. This is the realm of great cosmic loss. You are here, that is enough. You want to be here, and you've shown up at my door to offer your support. I don't care that you just said that slightly goofy thing. It's okay. Come on in.

There are many tips I can give you that can help guide a conversation about grief, but I want to acknowledge that, fundamentally, it's a change within you that matters. It can be frightening when someone feels so much rage, sadness, despair: it shows us our own vulnerability – that this could happen to us, we could be as stranded as this person is.

I have only become better at talking about death through dealing with my own emotional reactions. By being aware of my fear and its consequences – how it was asking me to avoid talking – I was finally able to breathe, stay and listen. Once you realise the griever just needs you to be here, you can stop trying so hard to do anything else. The more we practise holding the pain of others, the better we will be at supporting them. If we all take this level of care, people will feel less vulnerable in their grief. Imagine a society practised in expecting emotion from a griever, not asking them to pack it away or stop or leave; a vocabulary based on compassion, not fear. Eventually you can wind a ribbon of support around someone and weave a place where they can rest their grief-mess – briefly – just long enough to know they're not walking alone.

I've had so many people try and get it 'right' when talking to me. My favourite reaction was from the late, great Ken Campbell, a very eccentric performer and writer who I was working with many years ago. One day he asked me, as we were driving along in his incredibly messy 4x4, 'Where's your dad then?'

My cheeks flushed. Ken wasn't known for his empathy. 'Oh he's … dead,' I said. What the hell was he going to say to me now?

He paused and looked wistful and let out a snort, 'Huh, yeah, they have a habit of doing that, dads.'

I laughed. I laughed so gratefully. He hadn't changed the subject, he hadn't shamed me. He'd sat with me, briefly, in grief. 'Yep, that sounds shit.' I was always very grateful for that answer.

JASON HAZELEY

Comedy writer and podcaster. Jason's father died while living abroad in Spain.

I was in a pub in Shepherd's Bush with some friends, one of whom was [comedian and writer] Carrie Quinlan. I was talking to her about it, and she had lost her dad I think about two or three years before me … and she put her hand on my elbow, leaned in and looked me straight in the eyes and went, 'It's shit, isn't it?'

And I said, that's the most accurate thing anybody is going to say to me, 'It's shit, it's just shit.'

SALI HUGHES

Writer, journalist and podcaster. Both of Sali's parents have died and she lost a very close friend at a young age to sarcoma.

The other thing that people need to do – and this never fails to amaze me every time somebody has died on me, I've always been completely perplexed by this, why don't people simply say, 'Oh my god, that is fucking shit'? Just say, 'That is fucking bullshit I am really sorry that has happened to you, that sucks more than anything I can think of, that absolutely blows.'

That is all you have to say. You don't have to put a spin on it, don't try and come up with platitudes. Just say, 'Fucking hell that is horrible, that is really horrible, and you must feel shit,' because people just want to be heard.

You can't make it better; you can't make the grief go away. You can't bring anyone back from the dead. All that's left to offer is to steady your feet, hold fast and stand next to them. Even though they are in pain, you can stay a while.

ANNA LYONS
Author of We All Know How This Ends*, end-of-life doula and co-founder of Life. Death. Whatever. — an initiative to redesign the dialogue around death.*

Talk to people, just talk to them and sit with them. If they don't want to talk, don't talk, but sit with them, be with them, let them know they're not alone. Let them know that you can bear the unbearable for them. What they're going through is unbearable and by not being there, by crossing over the street, by ignoring them, by ignoring what's going on, you're letting them know that it's so unbearable that they can't even have somebody with them. Carry it for them, even if it's just for a little bit. Show up, keep showing up. Just be there.

KAYLEIGH LLEWELLYN

The night my nephew died — my memory of that night is just fragments, flashes of memory, of little snapshots of the night. One of them is ending the night, sat on my auntie's sofa with [my best friend] Matthew sat beside me, just staring at a wall and him staring at it too. And it was awful, but I wasn't alone. Those things mean so much.

That has always stayed with me. The simplicity of what Kayleigh's friend did. Your brain in grief tells you repeatedly, 'You're alone with this, no one understands, no one cares.' To choose to walk alongside someone on that journey is the simplest and most helpful thing you can do.

What do we fear will happen if we give space to grief? Has anyone ever reported someone crying and not being able to stop for the rest of their lives? Even Alice in Wonderland's tears didn't wash her away, they led her somewhere else. It's okay to find it hard to talk about. It's okay to feel frightened or nervous. It's okay to stumble, make mistakes, get it wrong, try again. What matters is your presence. What matters is that you try.

Social awkwardness and fear drive us to seek to contain grief, tidy it up, run away — as if tears were petrol and we're all holding matches. We need to get better at being uncomfortable, at not knowing what to say and admitting that we're scared. It isn't easy to help someone in grief, I can't say that enough. No quantity of wipes, bleach or antibac will save us from the chaos of it all. Only when we attempt (and possibly fail) to help, will we learn what's needed.

*

The Rough Guide to Helping a Griefster in Grief with all the Grief*

(*This may still be wrong for your griefster. All griefsters are different, and some griefs may be more weepy than others. Consult a professional if you're worried about your griefster.[3])

---

[3] Terms & conditions apply. No griefsters were fixed, but many learnt to adapt.

Here's a small and unfinished map to lead you and the person you love through the maelstrom of grief.

You will get it wrong

MARK O'SULLIVAN
Writer and actor. Mark's dad died when Mark was fifteen and his mum died when he was in his twenties.

About two or three in the morning my phone rang in the hotel room, and it was my sister and she said, 'Mum's not alive any more.'

I said, 'What?'

'Mum's not alive any more.'

If anyone's listening, and wondering how to say it, that's probably not it.

Yes, I've said it already but I'm saying it again because everyone always thinks, 'Oh, but not me, I'm really sensitive, I will definitely not say anything stupid.' This is a reminder than even if you are the softest, most adaptable, memory-foam-mattress of a friend, you will one day get it wrong. Griefsters (maybe look away now sensitive souls) are a bit ... touchy. (Harsh I know, but it takes one to know one.) Grief rips your skin off and leaves muscle and tissue open to the air. Your words land not on a thick skin but sink into sinews and bump into bones. It hurts when it's wrong, yet it's hard to get it right. Because you can't. So, always have at the ready: 'I'm sorry if I get this wrong ...'

'I want to help, but I'm not sure how, but I want you to know I'm here ...'

'I think I may have been insensitive when we were talking, I'm so sorry ...'

You can't make it worse

Anything you say may hurt us, but it will never hurt as much as the fact THEY ARE STILL DEAD. That person is dead. You can't make it worse. The worst has already happened. Please always remember this when talking to someone grieving. If they start to cry or seem sad or upset – they are. They are in pain. That's okay. They loved someone and now they're dead. You can bumble and stumble and make it uncomfortable, yes absolutely, but you CANNOT make it worse. You can't re-dead the dead.

Aim not for perfection but presence. It doesn't matter what you say so much as that you are there, trying to help.

So, just try ...

POORNA BELL
Writer. Poorna's husband, Rob, took his own life.

Despite going through such a huge bereavement, the societal conditioning of feeling awkward around death is so strong that my immediate reaction when I hear of another person experiencing a bereavement is that I should retreat into my shell like a snail and be as quiet as possible. Because I don't want to say or do anything that might intensify or add to this person's trauma. And then the other part of me – this is the part that I think was given more substance and form after Rob died, and is far more empathetic and wise – just gives me a proverbial kick and then the words just come out. If they don't mention their loved one by name, I ask what their name is, because that feels important and I see their countenance shift as they say the words, and that person is brought into the room just for a moment. I say, 'I'm really sorry to hear that happened to you.' Especially a suicide, people just don't know what to say and they don't say anything and that just makes you feel even more alone.

The griefster can name and remember everyone who tried, who didn't give up on them, who fought through their own uncomfortableness to try and reach out.

Your grief is not their grief

It took me a while to accept that the grief of losing a parent didn't trump everything. My pain was so large and so raw that if someone told me they were sad about a dog or a grandparent or even, I'll be honest, a friend, I didn't understand. I didn't see anything but my grief for many years because my pain was so painful. Surely there was no pain that could beat it?

A lot of us in the club can be guilty of this. Grief is a standing stone in front of your eyes, the sunshine just peeking around the edges. The change came when I listened to people on the podcast. I realised that grief was grief, that if you had a relationship with them, and they died, you grieved for them. That's it really. Whether that's a dad, mum, sister, brother, uncle, grandma, friend, colleague, cat, dog,[4] it's grief. There's no grief hierarchy: whatever your pain, it's worth a place, worth a conversation. No

---

[4] I don't mean to be flippant here, I know to some a pet may not seem such a painful loss, but I have spoken to some grievers devasted by the death of an animal and others totally able to deal with the loss of a family member. We are all unique beings and how we grieve and what we grieve for doesn't have to make sense to anyone but yourself.

one can or should belittle, or make you feel like your grief isn't griefy enough to join the club. Whatever your pain, it deserves a space, your grief is valid.

This is particularly pertinent when it comes to talking about miscarriage or early pregnancy loss. A common reaction is to ask how many weeks someone was when they lost their pregnancy, as if a number can set a value on their grief. They were pregnant, they worked out the due date in their heads, they imagined a future, they are grieving.

Perhaps you have (like me) heard a grief story and done the grief maths and thought, 'Well that doesn't sound too bad/too early/too hard/too painful/they were old/you did know they were ill/it was sudden ... ' That's okay, you are allowed to think these things, it doesn't make you a bad person. Don't let that make you feel wrong or ashamed. No learning comes from those feelings. It's what you do with the judgement that counts. Know that you may not understand their grief, but if they are feeling it, it's real.

Don't ask – do
We place too much pressure on the bereaved to provide the answers. Saying, 'If there is anything I can do...' doesn't help a griefster. When you've been bereaved your head is soup, you don't know which way is up. Someone has died, you don't know what you want or need. If you want to win massive club points,[5] just do.

What do you think they need? Are they in full practical mode, just wanting to deal with all the sadmin – calling banks, lawyers, insurance companies – can you help with that? Look

---
[5] These aren't redeemable against not dying, sorry.

at their house, what do they need doing? Bin-emptying? Food brought round? Kids picked up? Teabags topped up? Enough digestives in the tin for all the visitors? There are so many little things you can do when someone is in crisis. Doing them without asking is a priceless act of kindness.

JOEL GOLBY

My flatmate found out my mum had died, and he did the nicest thing for me. I think people forget to be nice to you when it happens because they get it out of their system by giving you the long, sincere text message, or like, 'Anything I can do?' And they are like, 'Okay, I've ticked that off my to-do list, I'm a good person.' And then you are burdened with all this crap, all this probate, and when people have done the, 'Hey just want you to know I'm thinking of you and whatever I can do to help,' people kind of forget to just be nice to you.

I came home, I'm not a tidy person, my bedroom was a mess – and he'd tidied it. It was truly one of the nicest things anyone has ever done for me.

[Pro tip: Don't ask, 'Do you want tea?' Just put the kettle on and make it. Wash your mug up afterwards for bonus points.]

How are you today?
The dreaded, 'How are you?' is too much for most griefsters to bear. How am I? Awful? Lost? Afraid? It's too big a question to answer. How are you *today*? is the magic friend you need. Pinpoint your question to make it easier.

Also, be wary of, 'I'm sorry for your loss,' the immortal phrase most griefsters are faced with after the initial death.

I don't mind it, it's all we have sometimes, but it is one of the most complained-about phrases I have come across. For me, it does something, but it can't just be a towel to mop up the awkward mess: it needs to be meant. I have never been offended when it was said to me with thoughtful kindness.[6]

You're a supporting role – not the lead
You can cry a bit, in solidarity, but wailing that you really loved them too means they'll have to comfort you. They might cry, that's allowed. You can cry, yes of course. Your feelings are valid but not as valid as the person bereaved right now. They are the focus and if you feel upset, find someone (not them) to help you with your feelings. It's their close-up and your job is to make sure the camera stays on their shot.

Contact them
There are so many ways to be in contact with each other these days. Silence really has no excuse. Send a card, send a text, a DM, a WhatsApp, an email. Let them know you're there. Then stay in contact. Text 'Thinking of you' when you remember them. It's such an easy way to remind someone that they're not alone.

Be okay being ignored
Someone is now permanently ignoring them, so they might need to ignore you. Wait. Be patient. After the first year, remind them they've survived.

---

[6] Feel for the Swedish who, when I was recording a *Griefcast* live in Stockholm, told me they don't even have a version of that phrase, they only have a very old-fashioned phrase that is the equivalent of saying, 'Dearest Sirrah, my sorrow passes to you at this moment,' so most Swedes don't use it. After the show, most of the audience and guests admitted they just don't say anything because they feel they don't have a phrase that does the job, so it's easier to say nothing. 'I'm sorry for your loss' isn't much, but at least we have that.

Be there for the long haul

After a while people think you're fine. When you're not. Birthdays, Christmas, spring flowers … all these things must be faced without that person. Remember this when dealing with a strangely uptight friend about their birthday party six months later.

Take them out, send a card, mention what they've been through, say the name of their person. Make a note in your diary of the death anniversary. Even just the month. A year later, message them: 'Hope April is okay, know it's a tough month.' Work out when six months will be and text them then too. The power of remembering can't be underestimated.

Start practising talking about it now

Just allowing death to be a part of your everyday conversations will make you better at talking about it with those in need. You can ask now, before someone is weeping about a death, on a day when they are fine – 'Who was that person? What were they like? Do you miss them?' Open the door to it.

Grief looks different every time

They might be smiling, laughing, back at work, on holiday, posting selfies, but they're probably not 'fine'. They might not be awful, they might be doing okay – but it helps to remember that grief is a visitor, it comes and goes. Just because you see a picture of a person choosing to present themselves as unaffected, it doesn't mean they are. It might just mean that's what they're needing to do for a bit to survive.

You don't need all the details

I know it's hard, I know every bit of you wants to find out what happened. That's human. But do you need to know everything? Do they want to talk about it? Some people find it very painful to talk about the details of a death, especially if it is still recent. As you practise having these conversations, think to yourself, 'Why am I asking? Is it to help them?'

During the pandemic, Covid-19 griefsters have spoken to me of their pain at being quizzed about their loved ones' illnesses. 'Did they really have it when they died?' 'Had they been tested?' 'Was that what they actually died of?'

These questions are not really about their person – they are about the questioners' fears. How much better would it have been if they'd said, 'God I'm so sorry. That's sounds so hard, what was their name? What were they like? I would love you to tell me more about them if you ever feel ready.' You can listen and give space to their dead person, as if the death wasn't directly linked to your own lifespan.

Suicide

Deaths that are wrapped in tragedy or traumatic events aren't just grief: they are trauma and grief combined. Suicide can be very frightening to talk about if you have no experience of it. Only recently have we felt able to discuss it as a society at all, and in some countries it is still an illegal act. The stigma for many suffering grief from suicide remains, but that does not mean the conversation should be closed down. How we talk about it is where the sensitivity must lie. It is recommended by Samaritans that when it comes to talking about suicide, as a rule, you do not need the details, you do not need to ask how it was done.

The rule with suicide is you don't ask 'how' — no one needs to know that information because it doesn't change the outcome. I find it grotesque and voyeuristic because people assign their own sense of morality and judgement based on the answer. When you are asking someone that question you are asking them about the most singular point of their pain, making them relive the moment they found out; the questions they have tortured themselves with about their loved one's final moments. But you can ask the person how they are doing. And you can ask them about the person they lost because, even though they died by suicide, that doesn't define that person's whole life.

Estrangement

Grief can also come when there has been an estrangement. When someone has made the choice to not see someone for many years, it can be easy to rationalise that their grief will be minimised. If they didn't get on with that person, if they'd fallen out with them, perhaps they won't be so sad? We may wonder this because we often look to apply logic to grief, to do the grief maths again, so once we have all the parts of the equation, we can place a value on how much grief *we* think they should have.

Grief doesn't come with a checklist that you need to meet to be allowed to grieve for someone. You can easily be estranged and still mourn their loss; you can hate them and still suffer grief. The idea that you only deserve to grieve for someone you loved or liked is too simplistic: relationships are complicated, people are too. Grief comes when it comes, it is never a reflection of how well you got on with that person; we limit our view of grief when we place such restrictions on it. If you feel it, it's there. It's never our job to value what someone else should be feeling. I have known people dissolve after losing someone seemingly not that close to them – we can never truly know what we mean to each other.

SALI HUGHES

I think it was a very slow grief. I suppose the only time I've ever kind of felt any parallels with a different situation is sometimes if I speak to somebody whose parent had dementia or Alzheimer's, where they have this very long, gradual, drawn-out process of grief and then someone dies. It's a bit like that. I think I had had lots of therapy, and lots of crying, and lots of rowing with her and all of that stuff. And so I think by the time she died I had done a large part of the grief over my mother.

Before they've died

The grief that can occur before someone dies, perhaps due to estrangement or even a degenerative disease like dementia, is referred to as anticipatory grief. You may begin grieving for someone as soon as they are diagnosed or if they start losing who they are due to illness. For some people that can mean they've already been through a large part of the grieving process for many years before that person dies; for others it's not that simple.

Anticipatory grief doesn't protect you from grief around the actual death; it may still come crashing towards you, after years of knowing that moment is coming. Or it may mean that when death finally arrives, there is a relief. Neither is wrong, there is only grief.

ROBYN HOLLINGWORTH
Writer. Robyn's mum died of cancer and a few months later her dad died of Alzheimer's.

When someone has been given a kind of death sentence, essentially, you're mourning from that point – you're grieving already. Especially with Alzheimer's, because it's taken the mind of the person that you love, all that's left is their shell, so you're grieving for that person already. So, the moment that the death actually happened I felt quite a huge relief. Especially with my dad, it was a kind of relief in so many ways. I felt relieved for him, he wasn't suffering any more.

Don't give up ...
On them. On hope for the future, on the idea that one day it will get easier. Stay fast if you can. They may be in shock. They may take years to realise how much it affected them. You can't save them, you can't fix them, but you can let it be known that you care. There is no escaping the empty tunnel you're both walking into – just remember only you can see the light at the end of it. They can't yet. Keep walking.

Jack Dee Isn't My Dad

I get asked to do a comedy chat show thing. It's a drive away – Dorset? Somewhere far in a long car journey. We meet at a station in south London and get bundled into a van. It's jollier than it sounds. The van is full of stand-up comedians, and me. I'm not a stand-up – I can't stand up and say, 'Hey have you noticed that ...' because every time I try, all that comes out of my mouth is, 'He died. He died. He died.' Instead, I write characters and hide in case the death chat leaks out. It's always leaking out. It's like a burst pipe in the attic that has been drip-dripping for years, the water finding its way into strange places, trickling down into actual life.

Jack Dee is hosting the show. He's kind and friendly (sometimes they aren't) and doesn't seem offended that I'm here (sometimes they are). I'm not great that night because I'm nervous, but he makes it okay and he's so good at his job, it's fun to do.

We drive back and I'm tired and I feel like a child being driven somewhere. I listen to the chat in the car. It's funny. Comedians are funny off-stage, it's nice. I look at Jack and I realise he's probably about the age my dad was when he died, a bit older maybe: a middle-aged man with dark hair. And I think, 'Oh, that's what dads look like.' You don't see many dads looking so dad-like in your day-to-day life. I don't see it. I haven't seen it for years.

He's fussing over us in a friendly way, he's asking about drop-offs, how this ragtag bunch who live in this massive city will get home. I notice he's worried about the girls. There are two of us. He's making sure we've got cabs booked from where the van is dropping us all off. Like a dad. I can't stop noticing it, he's checking we're okay. Like a dad would.

I get out in the midnight black of a dark wet London night. I march towards my cab, running from the rain. I turn round and I see that he's got out of the car to make sure I'm okay. He gives a perfunctory wave – all good, she's in – and he turns back to the van. I burst into tears. I can't stop crying as the cab drives away because that's what dads do: 'You alright? Got everything you need? All good then, see you soon.' And even though my dad wasn't nearly as normal as that, I recognise it, that feeling. A middle-aged man just checking you got in okay.

That's what you lose, that set of eyes looking out for you. I'm okay, I don't need it, but I had forgotten what it felt like and, just for a moment, it was lovely to have it back.

Wave — 2017

I am getting better, slowly. I can feel it. Parts of it have lifted. Not all of it, but it's not as heavy as it was. I carry it easier most days.

I have a baby now, a daughter. I am a mother, a parent to a brilliant, bright, tiny, fiery thing. The experience of birth brought me closer to my grief than ever before: my own vulnerability, human frailty and strength so close to each other. I never expected him to see this, but still, life moves on, still you feel it.

We have moved to a flat near parks; we're people who care about the nearness of parks now. We discuss how good slides are or whether the roundabout is safe. We have bought a flat. Who are we? Who are these people? I feel scared and privileged to have this much responsibility. We bought a flat because someone died. Of course. It's London. Either someone dies or you were already rich. Buying it was hard, painful. Every bit of joy and excitement of moving is sucked back into the black velvet bag the money came from. He frets. He doesn't want to waste her money. It doesn't feel like ours. It feels loanish, but no one will ever come to claim it back, and that's awful.

I don't like the flat, it's too high up, the floors are dark, which is depressing, and the kitchen looks like a log cabin. The night we move in I hear shouting from the park. I'm convinced gangs of youths are fighting a war there. A few days later I find out that it had been a late-night football practice, just middle-aged men heaving cold breath into their bodies.

My daughter is getting bigger, more solid. She's nearly one, more person and more personality appear with each new inch of growth. She smiles and I smile. My heart unfreezing itself. Slowly I am allowing myself to be warmed by her and not frightened by the change she has brought. I try and separate her from my grief. I feel how intertwined it all is: the urge to hold life still, to make it static so it can make sense. It's why photos are magic, why we stare at ourselves fixed in time. It gives us control, allows a pause in the spinning. The deaths and the births, the gains and the losses. Just endless chess, adding and taking away.

I am becoming her mother. I have learnt that it is a slow process to become a parent, just as it was slow to lose one. It took months, years, before the house unmoulded itself from him, before his study became the spare room, before the smell went, before it became the room with the cot for grandchildren to sleep in, the little room, not dad's office. It takes years. People who live for forty-four years don't disappear overnight. They fade slowly.

We're in the park. She likes the swings, sort of. Not as much as other babies. She's curious and willing to try, but not happy-go-lucky. She's suspicious and weighs things up carefully. I am used to the women in the park, the mums. The park is women and children, like a fenced-off lifeboat. Mums and aunties and nannies, chatting about weather and sniffles and where to buy good wellies. It's an easy female space that I have slotted into. I want to be one of those mums who says she can't do it, can't be at the park and face the chat, to be cooler than this suburban discourse. But I'm not. I'm quite mumsy. It feels weirdly easy sometimes.

Today an old man is here. He has silver hair and a bomber jacket — London won't let you age too fast. He is pushing a little girl on the swings; he's laughing but his energy is different to the mums and the aunties and the nannies. He pushes her high and doesn't look at the swing. The baby loves it. She shrieks with excitement, and at the edge of the park I notice a nervous grandma marching towards them. 'Careful!' she shouts. He's barely watching the child, she's flying about in the swing, but you can tell she's fine. It looks more dangerous than it is, like all dad moves. I can't stop staring though because it's a grandpa. A grandad. That's what they look like. That's what it's like. I stop and my breath disappears.

For a second, I see him so clearly: grey hair, not white; trainers; whizzing her about, throwing her too high, my mum shrieking, 'Pete be careful!' I hear her laughing and I see her looking at him, like I looked at my grandpa. My adored grandpa. I see her looking at him with that level of adoration and love and him noticing and not noticing. I see how proud he'd be of her. I can see him standing there in the park, in running trainers that need changing and a jacket from M&S that is surprisingly cool. I see it. I hear my mum's miffed expression, 'She's going to be sick, Pete!' I see her looking at him.

He's gone. There's no grandpa for her and I feel like I've let her down because I had one and he was great. She doesn't have my childhood, it's going to be different. That's okay, I tell myself. I stare at the white-haired man and I suddenly hate him. I hate him and his life and how lucky he is to push his granddaughter on swings and how I hope he fucking knows how fucking lucky he is to push her. I am staring. He looks at me. I dart my eyes away. I am being odd and not obeying the laws of the playground. They head off. I watch them fuss in the buggy as they walk away, a small unit discussing what their daughter and son-in-law are doing wrong. I yearn, I ache for that. My heart hurts to see a path that will never be mine.

But she is still smiling and jolly and trying to pick up leaves and being silly. She's funny and smart and sassy. I know he would have thought she was brilliant. I know it. There's no doubt in my mind. And that's something. To know she would have been loved, I can tell her that. I know how to love her. I was shown that. That's something. We haven't got it all, but we have some excellent bits. We leave the park and cross the field, dadless and grandpaless, but happy.

7

When You Die

KAYLEIGH LLEWELLYN

Heads-up: for people who might plan on dying someday, it's really nice if you let people know what you want at your funeral and what songs you want.

We're all going to die. The inevitability of it is almost laughable. It's like watching someone holding a large number of boxes head towards a banana skin, we know what's coming. I understand this truth well, yet it frightens me. It's a fixed point, the brightness of a star. What you're seeing as the light reaches you has already happened – we've already died, it's already a point on our timeline. But we still act as if it's not something we need to prepare for. Many of us struggle to talk about death in the abstract; confronting the reality of our own demise is more impossible still.

Have you sorted out your will? Don't feel guilty because – here's a terrible secret – neither have I. Me, Captain Grief,[1] talks about it all the time, advocates removing the stigma around death, constantly reminds people that it's going to happen, it will come to them. Yet I haven't sorted out my own will yet.[2] So I understand that it's harder than it sounds to actually take the practical steps towards preparing for our own mortality, the steps that could guide our loved ones later. Not just wills, but the

---

[1] Cape made of black crepe, and I can fire coffins out of my hearse gun.

[2] Probably going to do it now, now I've publicly shamed myself.

difficult and awkward conversations with those who love us, that we are too scared to bring up. What do we want to happen to our body? Do we want to donate organs? There's a wealth of preparation we could do. Why do we think we can wriggle out of this essential homework? Why aren't we having these discussions now, before sickness or an accident or tragic bad luck hits?

Death's simple inevitability is perhaps, paradoxically, what makes the prep so avoidable: it's going to happen, there's nothing we can do about it. The urge to throw your hands in the air, shove your head in the sand and pull the duvet over your head is real. But we know as club members that life is short. We know how precious our time is and how distressing and difficult the sadmin can be.

So, what can we do to protect the future grievers? We need to take a deep breath and start having the conversations. Not only will they help practically, but they can aid the grief process. The guests on my podcast whose relatives had made plans and talked about their deaths, spoke of their relief. The worst thing was happening, but they had a guide.

TOM PARRY
Comedian, actor and writer. Tom spoke to me about his nain[3] *on a live episode of* Griefcast.

My *nain* passed away and she planned her funeral to the letter. My mum and my auntie went home, and they found in her bedside drawer a little envelope and it had

---

[3] *Nain* is the Welsh word for nan or grandmother.

everything she wanted done. It was about four years old, and it literally said: 'I want these pastors …' She had three vicars she'd contacted three years before she passed away, saying, 'Just so you know, I'm booking you in to do a reading at my funeral … '

She'd planned everything, the hymns, everything, to the extent – none of us knew this was going to happen – but one of the vicars that she'd asked to do the service said, 'You don't know this, but she's written you a letter.' He got out this letter and read it from my *nain* just saying, 'I'm so proud of you all.' It was extraordinary. It said, 'I'm very proud of you, I've had a lovely life, thank you for the love you've given me, I've been so grateful.'

It was astounding. She was in a position to plan all that. There was a really lovely message at the end, where she'd written, 'P.S. Thanks for putting up with me', and everyone kind of laughed and cried. It was on her terms. She knew what she wanted. There's a woman that faced death with clear eyes.

You might not have the organisational excellence of Tom's *nain*, but you can at least talk. You can begin with the funeral conversation (cheaper and easier than anything legally binding). Just broaching the topic with a loved one may one day become extremely useful to them. If you can, gift them a piece of the puzzle solved, before the chaos of emotions descends.

Start with the basics. Think of it as the greatest party you get to plan that you will never attend. Do you want to be buried or cremated? What music do you want played? What food should everyone eat? Who isn't allowed to come? Who must be invited? My biggest tip as a person-who's-been-to-too-many-funerals: who can sing? Who do you know and love that can belt it out (in tune and with confidence)? Because you need to ask them now to a) come to your funeral, and b) stand at the front and lead the hymn/pop song/rap, because there is nothing worse than a load of shy funeral-goers who don't know the tune. It's a show, think of the audience! Okay, this might just be my particular hang-up as a performer who can't bear hesitant hymn-singing,[4] but, if you want to go out to an Aretha Franklin number, you're going to need someone with the pipes to deliver it.

When I do live recordings of *Griefcast*, I interview three comedians about their thoughts on their own death, what they want their funeral to look like and how they want to be remembered. It's always a fascinating conversation, and illuminating to me: the ones you might not expect to have a faith who do; the ones who can't bear to think of it; how many different versions of this same story there actually are. The comedian Tom Allen told me he wants a Victorian carriage with horses in feathered plumes. He doesn't want anyone looking happy because the least they can do is cry when he dies. Comedian Josie Long said she plans to prank her friends by having her coffin covered with advertising stickers for big companies like Amazon, so people would think, 'Wow we really didn't know her, did we?' (and have only one friend in on the joke, ready to reveal it all at the end of the funeral). Writer Andrew Hunter Murray hopes to have his ashes spread on his local tennis court to annoy

---

[4] I am happy to stand at the front and lead 'Jerusalem' if you have no one else who can.

the couple who regularly stay on the court longer than they've booked it for. Stand-up comedian Katherine Ryan said to just chuck her body on the side of the road; she doesn't care as she won't be there.

Whatever thoughts you may have had about it, tell someone: a funeral plan is a great way to invite death to the table, to initiate a conversation.

ANNEKA RICE
Broadcaster and artist.

I was hosting BBC Radio Two and Carrie Fisher had just died. And her coffin was in the shape of a Prozac pill. And I thought, 'This is the business.' So we started on the radio show this thing about, 'What would you put your ashes in?' And it became very creative and exciting, and everybody was talking about it. I've always said I'm obsessed with the colour blue – I'd like my ashes mixed up in some blue paint – and I thought, 'Maybe just even left in the blue paint with "Mum" written on, three pots for my three sons?' Then I took it one step further and thought: 'No. I'll ask a friend of mine who's an artist to paint three paintings using my ashes.'

The more I planned other people's funerals, the more I realised I had been too scared to think of my own. So I made myself. Drawing up a will takes some actual admin but telling your loved ones what you want is free and easy.

I want Handel's 'The Ways of Zion's Do Mourn' played at full volume as people come in. Have you heard it? It's an absolutely banging funeral track (it was written nearly

300 years ago for Queen Caroline's funeral, in 1737 – up there with 'Wind Beneath My Wings' for funeral tunes). I want a wicker coffin and, whatever time of year it is, I want to be buried with flowers that can slowly die with me. If it's winter I'll take snowdrops, Christmas roses and mahonias. If it's spring I want daffs, freesias and hyacinths. If it's summer, drench me in roses and sunflowers. I want to be in a nice outfit. I want to be buried with an excellent bar of chocolate, the expensive stuff. I want 'A Case of You' by Joni Mitchell to be played as I'm cremated, and I want to be scattered into the sea or a forest, whichever my loved ones decide is easiest for them to visit. I don't mind about the party – but make it a party. Play excellent music – dancefloor fillers – and make everyone boogie till their feet hurt. Serve cake in every flavour, bottles of wine but also nice non-alcoholic juices to remind people that I could only ever cope with one glass of the stuff. I want people to dance and laugh and say she was fun, she was kind, she was there for me, she was silly, we loved her. I want photos of me through the years on the walls so everyone can find a memory. I want people to leave with cake in foil and shoes in their hands.

Gods, spirits, faeries of the Underworld, know this: I want to live. I want to live long enough to have to revise my funeral plans as my friends will all be too creaky to dance. I want my death to not be frightening for my children, like my dad's was for me. I want them to have handrails to find their way through the grief fog. I want to be brave enough to give them that.

Funeral Chat Icebreakers ...

Buried or cremated?
Where should you spread the ashes?
Do they want flowers?
Do they want to be buried with something?
Who's a good person to ask when you get stuck with things?
Do they believe in life after death?
Will they send you a sign?
Should you make a memorial?
What poem do they want read?
What music do they want playing as the curtain creaks around the coffin?
Do they want people to be stood round the grave throwing earth in the pouring rain?
Do they want sandwiches or champagne?
Should people wear black or flamboyant colours?
Is anyone not invited?
Will they be cross if you invite them anyway?
What type of coffin do they want?
Mega-religious ceremony or lightly secular?
What should you tell the children?

How brave can we be? Can we take it a step further to the really difficult chats? What about your end-of-life care? What will that look like? Did you even know there were options? Are you happy to have your life support switched off if you're in some form of 'vegetative state' – have you ever discussed this with anyone? What about if you have dementia or a terminal illness, have you thought about what routes you would want medical staff to take with your body, even if they knew you were too sick to survive any treatment?

I know this is bleak, but if we can allow ourselves even just to think about it, to open the door a little to the deep fears we have about our own vulnerability, we can make death a less scary place to be. It's your body, your life, your loved ones. What help can you give them now, before they are standing in a hospital ward feeling desperate and overwhelmed? What would grief look like with that acceptance of death?

I met palliative care nurse Kimberly St John through *Griefcast*. Kim got in touch with me because she was on a completely amazing (and radical) journey to make death a subject we might want to talk about. When I first met her, she had organised a talk about death at a theatre and comedy festival in London. *At a theatre and comedy festival.* She'd booked me and three others. The event sold out.

I was staggered by Kim, her energy, her immediate compassion, her warmth. She made talking about death feel ... safe. I had been so focused on grief, a subject I felt comfortable with; however, I was more tentative when it came to death. If I'm honest, death still terrified me: myself dying, anyone I knew dying – my death anxiety was an ever-present visitor in my daily worries. But the way Kim spoke about death opened my eyes, allowed me to approach death more like I approached grief – as something that not only deserves investigation but can be interesting too. Kim wasn't dour or melancholy; when she spoke about end-of-life options her soft Welsh accent and huge smile shone through. She made me realise that not only did I need to talk about it all, but that it needn't make for grim conversation.

The main reason to talk about your death now is that options are available. When you give birth, you are encouraged to write a birth plan. Why not write a death plan so that you can tell those who are caring for you what you want at the end? An 'Advance Care Plan' (advance, not advanced) wasn't a phrase I'd heard until Kim mentioned that, not only had she made hers, but she'd also emailed it to her family. 'My dad thought it was a bit morbid,' she joked.

Despite the hurt I'd felt at my dad not talking about his death, I hadn't recognised my own equal refusal to look mortality in the eye. I felt the same as he did: I didn't want to think about it because, surely, that was telling fate I was ready. Kim showed me that you could make these plans now, from a place of calm, when your body was still your own, when morphine wasn't involved, when emotions weren't raw. She showed me what a difference it could make to the people you care about, what a difference that could make to the grief-messes we gift each other.

Brilliant, fun, full-of-sunshine Kim. She made death feel like another wondrous human process to take part in. She made me less afraid of the inevitable. She showed me that this was not only an essential, but a possible conversation.

Kim died in 2020 from a completely unexpected and very sudden stroke. She was younger than me, had just moved to a new house, just married. Her life was absolutely full of possibility. I found out about her death as I was idly pushing my child's buggy along in the park, my lockdown baby peacefully asleep, my headphones blaring out the *Hamilton* soundtrack. Her dear husband, Sam, sent me a WhatsApp to let me know. I stared at my phone in shock, sat down on a bench and wept. She was too young and too brilliant and too alive to die. I know we all feel like that; I know all our people were too good to die. But Kim, was ... well, she was in the walking angel category. And now she was gone. My death-chat pal.

Kim's death affected me profoundly, in a way I think both of us would have been surprised by. We weren't extremely close, we spoke every now and again, but she was sunshine in this world and, especially for those of us who do decide to face grief and death, to find a light in the grey grief-gloom is a most precious thing.

My chats with Kim had been about how people don't prepare enough. When death took Kim, I wasn't prepared at all. I was dumbstruck to be so harshly reminded of what Kim was always trying to tell me – that it will happen to us all. Kim had prepared for her own death; she had already made her Advance Care Plan and she had told her family and loved ones exactly what to do. Sam shared her ACP document with me, the very same one she had joked about emailing to her family. It's not inscribed on parchment or written with a quill. It's a simple, friendly-looking template document in which she straightforwardly expresses what she would like to happen in certain scenarios. In a section that asks why she is making this advance decision about her care, she wrote: 'I am a palliative care nurse who has cared for many people who have received treatments without any benefit, which have significantly lengthened their death. I want to die peacefully and with dignity – if possible.'

I often think of Kim's kindness and care, present even in this final act.

I spoke to Professor Mark Taubert, Lead of Advance Care Planning for NHS Wales. Mark is doing ground-breaking work to bring death chats into the light. He talked about how much fear there is, especially surrounding DNR (do-not-resuscitate) forms: how people worry that in signing one they might be being tricked out of receiving the treatment they need, rather than seeing a DNR as an honest contract between yourself and a medical professional, a way to stop your body being dragged through treatments that will only prolong the inevitable.

End-of-life care is a complex subject, but what Kim and Mark both focused on was the power of just thinking about your death, talking about it to a close loved one. 'Even snippets of conversations become important to doctors, nurses and the health care professionals looking after people at the end,' says Mark. He suggests that if you do get round to sorting a will, you appoint someone to be lasting power of attorney for health and welfare. That way, if anything happens, if you lose capacity, the person who you most trust can advocate on your behalf. There is even the possibility of video messages. If, for example, someone is suffering from motor neurone disease, they can record a video of their wishes while they are still well enough to do so and have it by their bedside so the doctors and nurses can 'meet' the person they are now treating.

If you are not in a hospital bed yet, there are various templates and websites that can help you set out your wishes.[5] These aren't legally binding, but they offer you a voice in a future moment when you might not be able to speak for yourself. After talking to Mark, I turned to my husband one night and, apropos of nothing, informed him that I didn't want to be resuscitated if my brain was f*cked. He wasn't overly thrilled that I had interrupted his settling down to sleep, but he's used to me by now. I started the chat, I took one brick down from the wall of protection. It felt okay – horrible briefly, and then okay.

There will always be situations where your wishes can't be carried out.[6] Anyone who has gone through the process of giving birth will know the wry look of an experienced midwife as you hand them your birth plan. What you want to happen and what needs to happen aren't always compatible. But now, more than ever, we are aware of quite how important and powerful the choices we do have can be. If we can begin to be brave and start these conversations, put something on paper, tell someone about it, we will not only be offering ourselves choice at a point when we wouldn't otherwise have it, but also invaluable support to the people we love.

---

[5] For more information see the resources section at the back of this book.
[6] Particularly during the Covid-19 pandemic, when so many goodbyes, last wishes and even bedside vigils were reduced to whatever technology could allow.

Anyone who has cared for someone dying knows the truth: there is no Hollywood ending. The idea that you will have your moment, that you will be able to even communicate if you are very sick or dying, is a fallacy we need to break. We must have these conversations now, while we live. Now is the time to talk about death, not when faced with it. Once it arrives, you want a plan for that wily bird. You want to be ready – as much as is physically possible. Some of us may be faced with the nightmare scenario of being the voice for a loved one who can no longer advocate for themselves. No one wants this to be true, no one wants to imagine it. But if it does happen, how much better to know you had an idea, even a vague one of what they wanted.

I know it's easier to look away, but listen to me: it will happen, whether you speak about death every day and let it be present in your life, or you never mention it at all. We are here so briefly, not all of us stay for a long time. Let us see death as part of the process, not an end to run from. Let us be courageous and acknowledge that the deal with life is that death will be the end.

We live, we die. That's it. Isn't it strange and normal? Isn't it awful and ordinary? Death doesn't have to be a fearful mirror you never look into. Think about it, talk about it, normalise it, accept it. Make your plan and let your loved ones know. And yes, I'm now off to write a will.

Questions from a Child

'When is ...,' she pauses and stares at me.

Four years old and always a question. *How far is space? Why is my name on the wall? Why do the bakers have to leave the competition? Why does wind make kites fly? How many is a million days?*

'When is ... everyone going to die?'

She asks it loudly. He is washing up, I am holding the baby and trying to jostle everyone into the living room to get them out of the way. I laugh because it's a funny question. 'I don't know,' I say. 'We don't know when it will happen, but we will die.'

She pauses. 'In a million years?' she says. She's smiling because I laughed and I'm grateful that I laugh in awkward moments.

Later I think, 'Was that right? Is that helpful?' ... 'Yes,' I tell myself, 'never lie, never say we won't die, never say it won't happen.'

Sometimes I say, 'I'll be here if you need me,' and I know it's not strictly true, parents sometimes aren't there any more. But I will be there, deep in your DNA. I'll be there. I'll do the only thing I can do — love you so hard that when I die you will still feel it, you'll know it. You were loved by me. You are loved by me.

He loved me. That I know. He loved me terribly, badly and brilliantly. I still feel it. When you're dead they can still feel it.

231

ADHD

A family member gets diagnosed with ADHD. It's not a total shock, he's full of energy, brimming to the top with it, a tornado in boy form. He's the one that looks like you. He's the one who can catch me off-guard when he's giving me a hard stare after I tease him for something. It's the brown eyes, like yours.

I start to read about ADHD – a friend has it, and another just found out she has it. I start to link articles together like knotted sheets thrown from a window. I climb up them and find you waiting, there in the room. My mum is dubious – everyone has something these days, she says. She says this whenever I tell her a friend has OCD or anxiety or mental health problems. She means it kindly. She is (like many of us) overwhelmed by the rush of letters that we can all now own, that were previously just a quirky part of your personality.

You had ADHD. It's obvious now. You, who would stay up to work till 4 a.m. without realising the time but couldn't sit still long enough to watch a sitcom episode. Always losing things, disorganised chaos in your tiny study – papers everywhere, folders, an entire office spilling out of a cupboard. I feel sad for you. You didn't know. I read a sentence describing undiagnosed ADHD in individuals as a loss of potential: whatever they do, it never quite gets finished or achieved and they don't understand why. That stings. You never said it, but I felt it. You weren't enough, doing enough, successful enough, enough enough enough.

I see another shard drop into place in front of the ones that shattered all those years ago. I rebuild you back into a person. A whole human. It takes years and years to pick up all the tiny pieces and fit them back into the hole you left. There you are, a little clearer now. That makes sense. The chaos, the stress, the manicness. I had always thought you were a forceful personality, laughed it off, imagined others lived with that level of tension in the house. But they had dads who sat down, dads who rested, dads who said, 'That's enough for today.'

I push now, I push and push and push because you taught me that. How you can push yourself to exhaustion and still stand. You once told me you'd learnt to sleep standing up on some mad course you'd been on. I didn't understand then – *Why would you do that? Why not lie down?* You grinned. 'I did it,' you said, 'I can sleep standing up.' The joy you felt at forcing rest to its most useless position, not even allowing your bones to sit for a brief moment.

'He would have hated to be ill,' they said. 'He would have hated to get weak,' they said. 'So, good that it was so quick.'

It's true. You would have.

I would have liked more time. But they're right, you would have hated it.

It's all true.

8

Get Over It

Why do I Still Feel Like This?

Dear future me,

Your father has died now, on 21st April 1998, as you know! It's coming up to 6 months, you feel a bit sad but numb — run out of tears. What's the point of crying now? He's gone, just need to move on.

Arguing with Ma. Fish dead. School — on top of for a change! Hope when you read this U R Happy.

Lots of love

past me xox

This is the first entry in my diary after he died. I gave myself six months before I thought I should be 'done'. Reading this makes me want to part the curtains of time, run back and grab that little girl so hard and squeeze her and tell her it's okay. It's okay to carry on grieving. It isn't meant to stop.

I know how I felt is common. I know many who have felt embarrassed, ashamed, confused that the feelings are not just … disappearing … after six months, one year, five years, twenty years. We've spoken about so many aspects of grief, the many cultural and historical reasons that we judge our grief, the ways you can help carry it with you, but I want to end on the wish so many of us have. When will the grief go away? When will I get over it?

It doesn't, you won't, AND that's okay.
(In case you needed to know that before we carry on.)

If you are at the beginning of this journey (I count the beginning to be one to five years after the death), hearing that you might feel like this forever sounds *awful* (being polite here – insert a stronger word if you need to). Because where you are currently, at the start of your grief, is probably a terrible place to be right now.[1] How can I reassure you that it will 'get easier' in one breath and that you 'never get over it' in another? Especially at the start, when you're raw and skinless, like the worst kind of chicken breast. How can never getting over it be bearable?

Let me tell you what 'not getting over it' looks like for me. First of all, today I am okay. Currently, twenty-four years in, doing a podcast about death on a weekly basis, and I am okay. My last death anniversary came and went. I was so busy on the day I didn't even think of it very much. It was there. A dull sadness in my bones, but bearable. This year's Father's Day was tolerable. I did my usual and tried to avoid social media, I allowed myself the spike of jealousy, and I let it pass (for fear of the nasty edge that seeps into me when I see a lot of pictures of 'Alive Dads'). Even as I write this book dense with grief, I am okay most days. There are days, hours, minutes, I still feel

---

[1] I found years one to five a blur of confusion, sadness, anger, weeping, crying – thinking, 'Oh I'm fine, I'm over it ... ' and then a slam back to a grief wave and the discovery I wasn't. For me, it was around year five that I felt able to raise my head a little and see how far I'd come. I hadn't been walking a straight path, more a Winnie-the-Pooh-like stroll around my own emotions, wiggling and retracing my steps in circles over and over again.

sad, I weep; I still feel my heart ache that I can't introduce him to my children. The sadness of the lost moments is there. But here, now, in this day, I'm okay. Not getting over it doesn't equal constant weeping: it's surviving, existing, not always in joy, but not always in despair. I'm not fine that he died. I'm not neutral about it. I feel sad to have lost my dad when I did, but my grief is faded and worn now, a part of me that I have learnt to accept.

What's hard about the beginning is that the waves keep coming, keep crashing over your head, tossing you upside down and slamming you into the sand. You're choking on grief those first few years. So, when a wave crashes down on you for the fifteenth time that day, you weep. Because when will it end? How can anyone live like this? But the longer time goes on, the further apart the waves become. Life seeps in between the gaps and, somehow, you're living again. Somehow you keep walking forward and what begins as a wave each week becomes each month, each year, every few years and, now, at my Grief Elder stage, there are many years between the waves.

The waves still crash. They just get further apart.

One of the joys of learning to live with your grief is how good you get at predicting the emotional weather. You learn when to look to the horizon to see the storms gathering and heading your way. You get better at understanding what's happening instead of being knocked over by it. The waves come. You learn to ride them. You get better at keeping your stance steady, shoving your feet into the sand to keep yourself upright, knowing this will not last forever. The wonder of living, of having so many years between yourself and the death, is that it allows resilience to grow along the way. You can look back and see you got through it then, so you can get through this wave and the next one too. Twenty-four years in, I've survived a lot of them. I'm okay.

It took me a long time to realise this, that it's like breathing; it's just something you will do. You will carry it with you, however aware or conscious you are of it. At many points I felt like the grief had gone. On year nineteen I felt better than okay, I felt 'done'. I could see how far I'd come from his death: so many things had happened, I had nothing left to say.[2] 'I won't ever feel that bad again,' I thought. I was 'over it'.

Then, on the twentieth anniversary of his death, I found myself falling to pieces.

April is my anniversary month. If you are in the club, you know the feeling of the date creeping nearer, looming towards you like some awful exam you've already failed. For me, the cold dread of anniversary fear starts in March. I begin to sense it in the distance – the month, the date, the time – galloping towards me like a Horseman of the Apocalypse on his annual holiday to Cariad-land. Then as April beckons, the countdown begins. Like a terrible Advent calendar, I'm ticking off the days before the 21st arrives. I've been doing this for years, always checking the horizon for its approach as we near the month, knowing that each year will bring its own anniversary energy.

---

[2] Hahahahahhahahahahahahahahaa.

239

For me years one to five were the worst[3] (shout out to years two and three for really putting in the work). The year-one anniversary was exceptionally raw: sitting in a school classroom as the clock wound its way round to 9.40 a.m., my heart beating faster; staring out through the large, clear plastic windows with graffiti compass-scratched onto them; head down on an A4 folder covered in cow-print fake fur. Staring at that clock, that simple utilitarian clock familiar to all schoolchildren, waiting, waiting, waiting, breathing for 9.40 a.m. to pass – just pass – be 9.41 a.m., be 9.45 a.m., be 10 a.m. Be gone. Then it's done. I can feel the cheap nylon under my face as I pretend to be lazy and asleep, one eye clock-watching till the moment has happened.

When it did, there was no explosion, no angels descending, the clock just ticked on. It passed. His time passed, he passed, the day passed, it just … happened.

That first anniversary is such a weight because for days before you're not sure how you will cope and then (usually) on the day, you just do. It just happens. You might cry, sob, wail. But you've been doing that all year anyway. So then you carry on as you have been and you realise, 'Oh this is it, this is life without them.' It just carries on. At least after year one you realise it won't destroy you.

I felt that first year very deeply: it felt visceral, I was there for every second of it. But after that, as I moved on to year six, year seven, year eight, I can't really tell you what happened, or how the exact moment felt. It began to blur

---

[3] Please remember, everyone's journey is different and if this doesn't fit yours, that is okay.

... until year ten. Ten was a shocker. Ten became TEN. A decade without him. Something metrically significant.[4] Those significant anniversaries, five, ten, fifteen, always felt louder. They required me to assess how much had happened since he'd gone. How much had he missed? Count it up: the king is in the counting house, counting out his money and memories and stories and jokes and discoveries that can't be shared any more.

Year fifteen felt hard for similar counts-of-five reasons, but after that, slowly, it began to become 'The Past'. The anniversary wasn't always easy, but it was quieter, a journey I'd now made many times. I knew what to pack, I knew roughly how long it would take me to get back home. How I felt about the anniversary, the day itself, changed. I began to think, 'I suppose this is it now' – a brief intake of breath, a wince as the day starts. I felt I had experienced everything the grief ride could offer. It had turned me inside out and back again and now, it was done, I was done. The grief was done.

This was reflected back at me when I spoke about his death to others. If I was asked how long it had been, I was able to reply, 'Oh, it was seventeen years ago ... it was eighteen years ago ... it was nineteen years ago ... Yes, a long time ago.' Their eyes would soften, and the tone and their gestures would imply, 'Yes, that was a very long time ago,' and they were 'sure I was fine by now', and I'd nod to show, yes, they were right, and we'd smile at each other. There would be no tears, no delving into the tragedy of

---

[4] Perhaps you don't get the same sting in imperial measurement countries: is twelve years worse if you live by inches and feet? Please tell me.

it, because it was all *a long time ago*. 'I'm sorry,' they'd say, then move on, like I'd told them I had once had a dog, once went to Berlin, I'd once spent a day doing an improv workshop with Niles from *Frasier*[5] – just a small fact from your past that was pleasantly interesting for a second.

Occasionally, this casualness would stop me in my tracks. Was it that long ago? Is seventeen years long? Shakespeare is a long time ago; dinosaurs are a long time ago. 'I remember my dad,' I would think. 'I met him. He was just here, he was just –'

But then the numbers would argue with me. 'Isn't eighteen years an adult lifetime away? That *is* a long time.'

They're right, of course it's fine now, it must be. People hadn't explicitly said, 'I'm sure you're fine now,' but the phrase hung in the air between us like celebratory anniversary bunting – 'Y-O-U-M-U-S-T-B-E-F-I-N-E-N-O-W!' – brightly coloured and swinging in the breeze.

I took this as evidence that others assumed I was over it: I felt okay, so therefore I was. This is what 'over it' looks like. A little numb. A little strange. You don't ever get to talk about them again. No one needs to know the details. They died. You're fine. The End. I had completed grief. I awaited my certificate and medal in the post.

2018. Twenty Years Since His Death

It had been happening for weeks, a slow unravelling of my control. The inner chaos I'd spent much of my life monitoring, politely asking it to sit down and behave, was

---

[5] FACT.

242

now thrashing around the floor screaming and foaming at the mouth. Loudly and unapologetically. The mad paralysing part of grief that hadn't visited me for years was now holding my feet to the floor. I felt like I was glued down, and yet all I wanted to do was run. Run away from this feeling. The creeping would begin in my feet and slowly grapple its way up through my body, like an endurance mountain climber, freezing me till I could feel it in my mouth. Grief.[6]

It hadn't been this bad for some time, that was what was frightening me the most. My waves had ebbed so far towards the horizon, I thought I was over the worst. I believed that. This familiar feeling of rising dread was terrifying me. I had forgotten its taste and its texture. I had become used to the anniversary passing me by, just glancing past me, nicking the edge of my skin.

It's February, yet the clouds are looming. But it's February? What are they doing here? February is Mum's birthday, Valentine's Day, winter's ending. I have no beef with February. Yet I smell beef. Steaming with gravy on a plate in front of me. I feel sick. As we get into March it gets worse, all I can hear in my head is: twenty years twenty years twenty years twenty years, over and over again.
2020202020202020202020202020202020202020202 0202020202020202020202020202020

Twenty of our years. Twenty. Years. Since he was here. Bloody twenty. It felt old. It felt too long, it felt wrong, it felt crippling. It felt significant in a way I didn't want to

---

[6] A bit like Elsa in *Frozen II*, when she goes too deep into the cave and she freezes as she discovers her ancestors weren't that great. That film is deeper on more levels than you are expecting it to be.

deal with. I tried to avoid it, sidestep it, dodge it, because I was past this point. I had finished! I had got to the top of the ladder! I had collected all the tokens!

But the clouds carried on rolling in. The sky was so heavy. I felt it as soon as I woke up. A lethargic crapness. Amid the pain, the sadness, the grief, what kept rattling around my head was a shock. That it was back. That the bloody grief was back. Again. That it could be this bad twenty years on. That this felt closer to what I had felt at year five than year nineteen. How had that happened? What had dragged me back into the past? Why wasn't I over it by now? Twenty years and yet I was still weeping, still thinking what-ifs. How? How can grief come back like this?

21st April. The Twentieth Anniversary of His Death

The day arrived. It was hot — warm for April. Pleasant, everyone kept saying. I felt my head suspended in a grey fog, muffled from life and any signs of living being a joyful thing. I knew I had to be alone; I knew that much about these kinds of days, a full grief day with no lunch break.

We lived in central London then, so I walked round the corner to the bike-hire stand tucked away off an old coaching road, juddered the bike and its heavy frame out of the rack and cycled off. I rode and rode and rode and let the thoughts pound out in my head. Before I knew it, we were at Hyde Park: me and my dad in my head. We were cycling round a park I rarely went to as an adult, but as a child had gone to weekly. He used to train here on Sundays for his various marathons and triathlons, riding and running and chatting and stretching; middle-aged men in Lycra and the clack of bike shoes on the concrete outside the Serpentine cafe; hanging out with my brother under cafe tables while grown-ups talked about running, meditation, Buddhism and Zen. There was a lot of Zen. Even someone's dog was called Zen – a spaniel that ran around hyper and overexcited, a perfect case against nominative determinism. We'd drive down with the bike strapped to the car like a stag from a kill, be here all Sunday morning. I remember the grass and the lake. Everyone struggling to get their wetsuits on, thick black pen numbering shoulders; numbers printed on square bits of paper, safety-pinned onto vests; running, cycling, swimming. He was so active here, so alive in this place.

He brought me back here today, to where he lived. Or did I finally let my thoughts guide me to somewhere that reminded me of him? It was nice. I rode out the whole day, did nothing but let myself think about what it would be like to have him around, how annoying that would be some days, what questions I'd tentatively ask him, what things he might tell me about. I sort of knew all the answers. I let myself ride and ride until I gently allowed the realisation to creep in that I wasn't bloody over it. I wasn't okay. I wasn't done. After twenty years I still couldn't say, 'Ah well, there you go, these things happen.' Why should I? Why should I be done because it's twenty years? Why should we – if it's not where we need to be?

CHARLIE RUSSELL

I'm not sorted, it was eleven years ago, and I should totally be sorted by now. Then I realised, 'Oh no, no it's the whole point.' People need to know that it is okay to be eleven years on and still working through it.

STEPHEN MANGAN

I just wanted to say to people: just try and deal with it as it comes along, and today you'll be dealing with something – you may deal with it well, you may not – and then tomorrow something else will happen, just keep trying. There's no right, there's no wrong. There's no successful. You're never going to beat it, never going to get rid of it. You don't want to get rid of it because you love them, you're going to miss them, so it's just to give yourself a bit of a break … Take it one step at a time … You can't wrap it up, there's no end result. There's only a continuing ongoing … that's what life is: you never 'get there'.

A few years ago, I was interviewed on a podcast about my work on *Griefcast* and the familiar question was put to me by the host: 'How do you help people get over it?' He was well meaning, he wanted to end on advice that would help listeners.

The twenty-year anniversary had finally taught me the lesson I needed: you don't. You don't get 'over it'. It might get easier, it might not; it will appear, it will go; it will be an ever-present presence in your life – just as the person was. It has taken years, but I have come to terms with the bleakness, the truthfulness and the freedom that the recognition of this has given me. Realising that grief can't be locked away has freed me. Now I don't fight my mess, don't hide it or suffocate it. It walks beside me with all my memories and lessons, freely. There's a peace but there's not an ending.

'You don't get over it,' I said.

This was not the quippy, uplifting answer he wanted. 'Maybe that's just you, right?' he quickly countered. 'You were really close to your dad. I think most people get over it?'

He wasn't asking, he was telling me, because what I'd said was frightening. I could even see he was starting to panic a little. 'No, it's not just me,' I explained. 'It happens to everyone, all these people, everyone I've interviewed, we all basically say the same thing. In varying degrees, we're not over it, we live with it. We live, we live happily and with joy but, no, we are never *over* it.'

He paused and gave me the stare of someone very much outside the club, a look I had received before ... *She's probably a bit weird, perhaps she had an odd relationship with her dad,*[7] *perhaps she's overdramatic.* He shook himself, relaxed. 'Yeah, I don't think I'd feel like that,' he said with the confidence of a man with both parents alive and well, and swiftly changed the topic.

In moments like this, when non-club members try to make rules for what your grief should look like, I have to fight the urge to scream: 'YOU'LL DIE TOO, THEY'LL ALL DIE, ALL THE THINGS YOU LOVE,' into their faces. It's why I have to be careful who I talk honestly about my grief with, and also why I am not allowed at parties any more. He didn't understand, why should he? He didn't have a grief-mess to carry. My scrappy dog that runs just behind me reminding me that time is limited, life is precious, that nothing really matters – he didn't have

---

[7] I mean I did, but that's not why grief doesn't end, honest.

that. He hadn't had the pain and the weeping either – and he didn't get the lesson.

It took a small breakdown, a bike ride and finally some therapy for me to understand I wasn't 'over it' and I probably never would be. If grief could come back at twenty years, it was probably going to come back at twenty-five years and thirty years too (as my predictable wave-schedule goes).

This was crushing at first, really and truly crushing, but like all good moments of destruction, it allowed new thoughts to grow through the rubble. I would never be 'over it', but I could be okay. My failure to move through the grief and reach a place of no emotion wasn't realistic, it wasn't how humans felt things. I was searching for numbness, to feel nothing, no grief, no pain, the emotional range of a robot. Obviously, every situation is different. I was dealing with a very specific case of teenage grief and shock that hadn't been processed. I'd placed such a huge pressure on myself to be rid of it all, of all the mess and the emotion and the feeling, when in fact allowing it to rise to the surface when it needed to, letting it be a part of my life, was the only thing that gave me the relief I was so desperately searching for.

The waves do get further apart, but they can still come crashing down on you, and yes, that's scary, and of course there are some days I hope I will never have to see one again. But I can accept that *this is grief*. This is what grief is, those waves, the space between them – all of it – it's just what happens when someone dies.

Grief psychotherapist Julia Samuel used a phrase that really stuck with me. She said of living with grief, 'It hasn't destroyed you, but it's shaped you.' There was a time when I would have found that very hard to accept. I didn't want to be shaped by it. I wanted to deny it had happened. I wanted to be seen as a perfectly normal person who happened to have a dead dad, nothing but a footnote in my story.[8] As the years rolled on, especially as I approached a decade since his death, I thought there was something almost distasteful about being shaped by it, still being sad about it. I regularly get emails from griefsters saying, 'I know it was a long time ago but, I know I should be over it but, I should, I should, I should but I'm not, I'm not, I'm not ... '

I have been shaped by it, by this pain. (It used to make me imagine myself as a black-clad babushka, trotting house to house, my black lace veil dragging along the ground. 'Here comes the Grief Witch,' they'd cry, as I trailed into the village on a carriage made of bones, pulled by half-dead hounds straining to stand, the sun clouding over and skulls falling out of my many unidentified pockets.) I used to be terrified of what it meant to be so affected by something that had remoulded the very shape of who I was. But now I see it as one of many significant events that have formed me. This one is a pain I carry; others are happy. All of them make up my life experience, make up me.

MICHAEL ROSEN

Poet and writer. Michael lost his son Eddie to meningitis when Eddie was nineteen. Michael also recently nearly died himself of Covid-19.

---

[8] Footnote about a footnote. If I could footnote this, I would.

I can't say to be absolutely honest that I grieve for him in the exact same way I did for the first few years. What I do now is think about him, and though I'm sad about it, I wouldn't call it grief because grief for me is … it feels to me that that is when you are at your most helpless and most vulnerable. So, I've parked grief … it's moved into another place, so it's not what I used to have when I thought about him. It feels safer; it feels like I can talk about it and think about it and live with it – and think about how he was in a way that doesn't leave me helpless.

I am not in pain daily. If I had to be precise, 17 per cent of my year currently is quite griefy. A large part of it isn't. It's happy, it's joyful, it's nice – but I am aware of my grief. It's different to what most people imagine the club to look like, what the podcast host was afraid of – a bleak life – David Lean does Dickens bleak. Some days are harder, but it is not a complete wasteland of tears, it's subtler than that. With time this is the same for most people. The proof is all around us: people in grief, next to grief, remembering grief, but still at Tesco's having a chat with you and laughing at the man who just fell over.[9]

In grief, you will smile, you will kiss someone, you will get on a plane, you will laugh – you will wear the clothes that you wore to their funeral to the pub one night and make a joke about it; you will go to university, you will get drunk, you will dance; you will have too much wine, eat

---

[9] He's alright, don't worry.

Chinese takeaway, watch *Strictly*; wear shoes that hurt, eat ice cream, go on holiday; fall in love, stay up all night, get married, have jobs, leave jobs, get new jobs, have a child, make new friends who don't know what happened; move house, move areas, cry, laugh, breathe, smile, scowl; get the tube, and wear the wrong coat for the weather, but still be glad you took an umbrella, just in case – and no one will know you're grieving. You will carry it inside you like a tiny fire that will not be put out. It will accompany you everywhere, like your thoughts do.

There are days when I don't think of it, and days when I do. I have learnt to let it pass, to feel it when it arrives and ask no more of it than that. It isn't possible to make it go away, but it is very possible to live with the pain inside you and to be okay with that – for both pain and happiness to be in one body at the same time.

KRISTOFFER HUGHES
Death service professional, drag queen and Druid. Kristoffer's nain passed away in 2021, his father in 2011 and his younger sister, Rachel, in 2009, when she was twenty-two.

There are times when I close the fridge door – and there's a photograph of the four kids, the four of us together, and there are just times when you feel that all of that emotion, all of that pain, is tethered down: it's anchored down somehow. And then years later it just takes a glimpse or a memory or a smell or a song to untether those ropes that hold everything down and you can hear them ping and the pain comes back. But now I've learnt to embrace that pain. When that pain comes, I allow it to overwhelm me, I allow it to cause me to cry. Because I hear so often, the words I hear so often as a celebrant, 'I don't think I will cope, I don't think I can cope ... '

My answer to that is always, 'Then don't. Don't cope. Stop coping.'

And do you know what happens when you stop coping? You cope. It's the bizarrest thing. I realised that the beauty of it all was the not coping, and now it's okay. If I want to cry because Rachel's no longer here, I cry. But the crying is a beautiful thing because it's indicative of the depths of love.

Fried Eggs Make Most Things Better

When I saw the 'ball in the box' theory (sometimes known as the fried egg theory), in a BBC video that has been shared millions of times on Facebook, I was a bit staggered. I had never seen a drawing that so clearly showed what I'd done with my grief, a visual metaphor of what so many of us do with grief without realising it. The ball in the box and fried egg theories are subtly different but have the same principle at heart. I really like fried eggs, so I'm drawn to that version, but if you like boxes you can choose that too.

What struck me about these analogies is how our views of grief have changed in the mainstream. Thanks to the power of social media, we no longer wait decades for these theories to filter down. The ball in the box theory went viral when Lauren Herschel, a griefster herself, shared it on Twitter, after her doctor had outlined it to her. Essentially the idea is that your life is a box, and when someone you know dies, it's filled with a giant ball of grief.

Inside the box is a pain button, which, when your grief is massive, it will continue to hit. Over time the grief will diminish but it can still randomly (the smell of a perfume, their song playing, a man in a suit on the tube ...) hit the pain button and cause you anguish. Several of my podcast guests have referred to this not as a pain button but as a grief ninja, or grief tiger, that can come and pounce on you when you least expect it.

The BBC video shows a similar diagram but this time the circle is your life. When a grief affects you, your whole circle (life) is filled with it; there's no aspect of your being that isn't affected by your grief. We used to think that over time the grief would shrink and disappear, the video explains, but now we mostly accept that the grief stays the same and your life (circle) grows around it. This was a revelation so large for me, I felt like a peasant standing in front of Galileo, squinting as he explained that the sun wasn't circling us. How I felt wasn't completely unique to me; other people, academics even, agreed that this is what grief can look like. The grief remains, it doesn't disappear.

When I saw that video, I felt a release. I wasn't holding on to pain, I wasn't doing something wrong. The grief may blur and change and soften over time, but it remains. Your grief-mess stays with you. You grow your life around it. That's what 'time heals' means; that's what they mean when they say 'try and live', 'try and get out there', 'don't dwell' – but none of these sentiments echo the whole truth. Try and live, because now you have a grief-mess to carry and that's hard to do. Make some life to grow around it, that will help. Now you have a huge grief ball to deal with, go seek joy where you can, but be gentle with yourself, because the grief is still with you.

For so long the way we have tried to help each other has been to sweep away the grief, to search the horizon for when it will disappear. It won't. We will always be going around the sun. You can't stop this physiological, psychological, emotional journey. You don't have to. It will just happen, it will just be there. And as we learn to accept the sun rises, a new day occurs, here I still stand with my grief and yet the world continues, we see the truth and beauty of life itself. The sadness, the death, the pain, the joy, the bittersweet agony of our own existence, it's all part of it. Your grief-mess isn't separate from you or the good bits of your life – it's just life, it's who we all are. We don't need a special bag for it, or a way to destroy it. It's always been there, you were already in the club, you just didn't know it yet. The club is life – people die, people live, people make you laugh, you keep walking forward. It was ever thus.

But now we know, grievers, griefsters, the ones who 'get it', club members, we know. We are blessed, and we are lucky. We know what death is, we know what it means, we know what forever looks like. We live in the most truthful place now; it is bright and it is cold. You can feel the air in your lungs and know that it, too, is not yours forever. We can take the waves crashing over us, because we know, nothing lasts forever.

Wave – 2021

January. Nearly a year into pandemic life. It has felt like grief. The quietness, the world stopping. All I ever wanted when he died was for the world to stop. How dare people shop and laugh and watch films and eat burgers, when he's dead. I wanted the sky to pause and the clocks to hold their breath and everyone to take a moment to acknowledge the terribleness of what had happened. But it didn't. The world ticked on – and later I was so glad that the river outside my door kept flowing; I could look at it and know that life goes on.

Lockdown feels as though Grief has taken over – it's in charge like some Greek god punishing us for disobedience, sentencing us to an eternity of stopped clocks and silence. The world frozen. It's like all the grieving people have been given what they asked for, only to find out it's awful – it's awful when you can't go shopping, hear the laughter, watch films and find yourself staring at other people eating burgers messily. It's awful and it feels like grief. I don't see my mum for three months. Every time I open the shoe cupboard and catch a glimpse of the slippers she keeps at my house a shot of adrenalin rushes through me, it feels like she's gone. I know she isn't. I know I'm lucky, but there's a horrible stench of grief, of loss, and I hate it.

February. The initial awfulness has faded to a stubborn blank acceptance. I feel like I understand people who lived through the war. I feel like I really know how long a year is. Years from now my children will probably tell me to forget about it, it was ages ago, it wasn't that bad. But I'll know it was really quite awful to live with grief in charge.

I am lying on the sofa trying to find five minutes of quiet. I am half asleep. I can hear my children in the kitchen: the two noisy people who fill the house now, the KIDS. The sky is pale, airless, still. Everyone is praying that 2021 delivers more than 2020 took away. But I know grief doesn't work like that. It's just the beginning for so many people. I watch it unfold in my head as I listen to the radio news: forty-four, forty-five, sixty-five, seventy-five, ninety-eight thousand thousand thousand thousand.

I close my eyes and hear a voice.

Who's that? In my head I'm back home – Mum's house. There is a grey mist in front of me; a slash of light opens vertically, like a gateway to the past on kids' TV. The voice is coming from the breakfast room. I can see downstairs through the door, I can see the banisters that we climb on and slide down. The voice again. I'm asleep but lucid enough to know if I search too hard it'll go. I just let the voice be there, and it's you. There you are. Your voice. I haven't heard it for so long. Is it because I had a son? Typical of you to only turn up now. I can hear you saying something urgent to us, saying something and laughing, the energy in your voice, hear you limping down the hall, one leg permanently shorter than the other thanks to that motorcycle accident that didn't kill you. I can hear you. I am so grateful that grief gifts these moments. That I am

256

alive long enough to be gifted one – to finally hear you after four years of complaining on a podcast that I couldn't remember what you sounded like.

The gap in the cloud is shrinking. I calm myself, I ask for a few more seconds. I hear you. And then, inevitably, the cloud zips itself up and I can only hear my children. I am being called, commanded to stop dozing and do something – play, bake, pretend to be a fairy unicorn. I don't feel fixed or even happy, I just feel calm, relieved I haven't lost you, that you are still here. There's a lot of noise, so I may not always be able to hear you clearly. But you are still here. That's nice. Today that's nice.

The Griefster's Protest

What do we want?
A SPACE TO TALK ABOUT OUR GRIEF!

When do we want it?
WHENEVER WE ARE READY AND IT'S AN OKAY
DAY TO TALK ABOUT IT!

What are we?
NOT ALONE!

What would also be helpful?
BISCUITS.

Dear Griefster,

We are here at the end. Sorry – I know we're not great with endings. How about, this isn't an end, it's just where we say goodbye, till next time, au revoir, adieu, auf wiedersehen, but no one died, so I'll see you soon.

If you need to you can pick the book up again and start all over; you can flip through the resources section and find some help there; you can have a look at the books about death and grief; you can listen to the episodes; you can tweet @thegriefcast and find me and all the other griefsters there.

Whatever your grief, whatever strange and manifestly painful road you've walked down, whatever life threw at you and continues to throw at you – look around you. We are all here. Some of us got here early and put out the nibbles, some of us are stumbling in very late, amazed the club even exists; others are waiting at the door, just looking through for years and years until their grief gives them permission to enter. But we are all here. The club is full to the brim with all of us.

We will all experience grief. We will all experience loss. Your first big loss will shock you out of the safety that life has no limits. Each loss after that will teach you something new, it will never be easy, it will never be pleasant, but it will always be truthful. It will show you what matters, it will show you who cares, it will show you what you want to be, who you are, who they were, it will keep teaching you lessons and keep remoulding you.

It won't disappear, it will fade and grow and get bigger and smaller and the mess will be only yours. People can carry it for a bit and ease the load off you, but mainly you will hold on to it and learn when it's useful and when it's painful and when it's just fine to be sat next to you.

If you're reading this and you're new to the club, don't let my twenty-plus years of grief scare you. I'm happier now than I ever thought possible. I have lived and lived and lived and carried all the grief with me, and actually, it's been fine. Never easy but honestly fine. You will get through this. You will find things to smile about, your heart won't always hurt. You will have good times again, you will. Because we do. Just look at the evidence of what people can get through, that's the answers you need right there.

Look around at all the joy and all the grief and all the mess people carry with them. We're all just basically trying to do our best with the time we have – it's never enough, we will always want more of the good stuff with the ones we love, but if we have enough memories and love, it can keep us going for longer than you might expect.

There are no last words, no pithy way for me to wrap this up. It's a mess, it gets everywhere, it affects things you don't think it will and jumps up when you don't want it to, but eventually you get used to it, and you get better at calming it because you let it be and stop fighting.

I hope you are as okay today as can be expected. I hope you're having an okay week. I hope somewhere there are things that feel okay. I hope you have cake and tea and comfort and someone to message if you need to. I hope you know this will pass, whatever you're feeling right now, joy or grief, will pass; it all eventually blows away. We aren't special or different, we just chose to acknowledge that death is in the room, part of the furniture, we dust it and put it in a place that feels right for now.

I hope you found the book helpful, I hope you're supported, I hope the pain eases.

You Are Not Alone.
Cariad x

you are not alone.

Grief Resources

There is a wealth of support out there for people grieving – never, ever feel like there isn't help. You might not want it yet, it might take time to find the right service or person, but one thing I have learnt by talking about grief is how many people there are out there willing and trying to help people through.

Here is a small section of different organisations and resources I've found along the way that have been helpful. Much love to you.

BOOKS

Gary Andrews, *Finding Joy* (John Murray, 2020)
Chimamanda Ngozi Adichie, *Notes on Grief* (Fourth Estate, 2021)
Flora Baker, *The Adult Orphan Club* (Flora Baker, 2020)
Richard Beard, *The Day That Went Missing* (Charnwood, 2018)
Poorna Bell, *Chase the Rainbow* (Simon & Schuster, 2017)
Candice Brathwaite, *I Am Not Your Baby Mother* (Quercus, 2020)
Kayo Chingonyi, *A Blood Condition* (Chatto & Windus, 2021)
Ruth Coker Burks, *All the Young Men* (Trapeze, 2021)
Reverend Richard Coles, *The Madness of Grief* (W&N, 2021)
Emily Dean, *Everybody Died, So I Got a Dog* (Hodder & Stoughton, 2019)
Megan Devine, *It's Ok That You're Not Ok* (Sounds True, 2017)
Atul Gawande, *Being Mortal* (Wellcome Collection, 2014)
Joel Golby, *Brilliant, Brilliant, Brilliant Brilliant Brilliant* (Mudlark, 2019)
Jayson Greene, *Once More We Saw Stars* (Hodder & Stoughton, 2019)
Gavanndra Hodge, *The Consequences of Love* (Michael Joseph, 2020)
Lee Lawrence, *The Louder I Will Sing* (Sphere, 2020)

C. S. Lewis, *A Grief Observed* (Faber and Faber, 2016)

Kat Lister, *Elements: A Widowhood* (Icon, 2021)

Anna Lyons and Louise Winter, *We All Know How This Ends* (Green Tree, 2021)

Helen Macdonald, *H is for Hawk* (Vintage, 2014)

Charlie Mackesy, *The Boy, the Mole, the Fox and the Horse* (Ebury Press, 2019)

Kathryn Mannix, *With the End in Mind* (William Collins, 2017)

Diana Khoi Nguyen, *Ghost Of* (Omnidawn Publishing, 2018)

Séamas O'Reilly, *Did Ye Hear Mammy Died?* (Fleet, 2021)

Olivia Potts, *A Half Baked Idea* (Fig Tree, 2019)

Sophie Ratcliffe, *The Lost Properties of Love* (William Collins, 2020)

Jack Rooke, *Cheer the F**k Up* (BBC Books, 2019)

Michael Rosen, *Many Different Kinds of Love* (Ebury Press, 2022)

Julia Samuel, *Grief Works* (Penguin, 2017)

Sara Seager, *The Smallest Lights in the Universe* (Fourth Estate, 2020)

Nikesh Shukla, *Brown Baby* (Bluebird, 2021)

Kate Sutton, *Drawing on Grief* (Leaping Hare Press, 2022)

Robert Webb, *How Not to Be a Boy* (Canongate Books, 2017)

Felix White, *It's Always Summer Somewhere* (Cassell, 2021)

CHILDREN'S BOOKS

Julia Donaldson and Rebecca Cobb, *The Paper Dolls* (Macmillan, 2012)

Samuel Langley-Swain and Katie Cottle, *Storm in a Jar* (Owlet Press, 2021)

Stephen and Anita Mangan, *Escape the Rooms* (Scholastic, 2021)

Jayde Perkin, *Mum's Jumper* (Book Island, 2019)

CHARITIES

The Alder Centre – providing bereavement care and education for anyone affected by the death of a child at any age: https://aldercentre.org.uk

AtaLoss.org – helping bereaved people find support: https://www.ataloss.org

The Brain Tumour Charity – https://www.thebraintumourchar
ity.org

CALM, Campaign Against Living Miserably – https://www.thec
almzone.net

Child Bereavement UK – helps children and young people (up to
the age of 25), and families, to rebuild their lives when a child
grieves or when a child dies: https://www.childbereavemen
tuk.org

The Compassionate Friends – a charitable organisation of
bereaved parents, siblings and grandparents dedicated to the
support and care of other similarly bereaved family members
who have suffered the death of a child or children of any age
and from any cause: https://www.tcf.org.uk

Cradle Charity – support for anyone after early pregnancy
loss: https://cradlecharity.org

Cruse Care – bereavement counselling, online help (https://
www.cruse.org.uk) and helpline. I've had many friends and
family who've accessed their services and loved them. They
normally offer between one and six sessions of face-to-face
counselling. They are also really active on Twitter, so do tweet
them @CruseSupport to try and get help there

Edward's Trust – Birmingham-based bereavement charity
supporting children, young people and their families: https://
edwardstrust.org.uk

The Good Grief Project – understanding grief as a creative and
active process: https://thegoodgriefproject.co.uk

The Good Grief Trust – bringing bereavement services together
so you can find tailored support: https://www.thegoodgrieftr
ust.org

Grief Chat – free, professional support through grief with a
qualified bereavement counsellor: https://griefchat.co.uk

Grief Encounter – give every child and young person access
to the best possible support following the death of someone
close: https://www.griefencounter.org.uk

The Grief Network – a community by and for young bereaved
people, who run meet-ups and events in London: https://
www.thegrief.network

Irish Hospice Foundation – https://hospicefoundation.ie

Let's Talk About Loss — a safe space to talk through taboos and address the reality of losing someone close to you when you are young: https://letstalkaboutloss.org

Life. Death. Whatever. — an empowered approach to death, dying, life, living, illness, adversity and grief (also amazing on Instagram, see below): https://www.lifedeathwhatever.com

The Loss Foundation — Providing free bereavement support for loss from cancer or Covid-19: https://thelossfoundation.org

Maggie's — a charity providing free cancer support and information in centres across the UK and online: https://www.maggies.org

MIND — mental health charity: https://www.mind.org.uk

Missing People — https://www.missingpeople.org.uk

Modern Widows — https://modernwidowsclub.org

Muslim Bereavement Support Service — https://mbss.org.uk

MYH, Muslim Youth Helpline — https://myh.org.uk

Nafsiyat, Intercultural Therapy Centre — https://www.nafsiyat.org.uk

The New Normal — changing the way we discuss our grief, mental health and well-being in open and honest spaces: https://www.thenewnormalcharity.com

Papyrus, prevention of young suicide — https://www.papyrus-uk.org

PCPLD Network — palliative care for people with learning disabilities: https://www.pcpld.org

Petals Charity — providing specialist counselling after baby loss: https://petalscharity.org

Pip's Kit — helping children who have a parent or carer with an incurable disease: https://www.pipskit.com

Samaritans — just the most wonderful organisation. If you feel overwhelmed or if you just need to speak to someone now, please do call, text, email or tweet them. There are people waiting to listen 24 hours a day: https://www.samaritans.org

Sands — support for stillbirth and neonatal death, through bereavement support, research and campaigning: https://www.sands.org.uk

Saying Goodbye — information, advice and support for anyone who has suffered the loss of a baby at any stage of pregnancy, birth, or in infancy: https://www.sayinggoodbye.org

Sudden – help when someone has died suddenly or too soon in their life: https://sudden.org

Sue Ryder Trust – palliative, neurological and bereavement support: https://www.sueryder.org

Suicide & Co. – support after suicide bereavement: https://www.suicideandco.org

Survivors of Bereavement by Suicide: https://uksobs.org

The Swan Song Project – gives people living with terminal illnesses or dealing with bereavement the opportunity and support to write and record their own original song: https://swansongproject.co.uk

Twins Trust Bereavement Support Service – exists to support all parents and carers of twins, triplets or more who have died, whether it was during or after pregnancy: https://twinstrust.org

Untangle Grief – bereavement support: https://untanglegrief.com

Way Up – online widowed support group: https://way-up.co.uk

WAY, Widowed and Young – https://www.widowedandyoung.org.uk

Winston's Wish – support children and their families after the death of a parent or sibling: https://www.winstonswish.org

ONLINE

Instagram
60 Postcards – @60postcards
Gary Andrews – @garyscribbler
Zoe Clark Coates – @zoeadelle
Cruse Bereavement Support – @crusesupport
Fandangoe Kid – @fandangoekid
Going With Grace – @going_with_grace
The Griefcase – @thegriefcase
The Grief Gang – @thegriefgangpodcast
Grief Kid – @griefkid
Grief Network – @greifnetwork
Grief Tips – @grieftips
Mark Lemon – @marklemonofficial

Life. Death. Whatever @lifedeathwhat
Lockdown Grief – @lockdowngrief
Modern Loss @modernloss
Charlie Mackesy – @CharlieMacksey
The New Normal Charity – @tnncharity
Julia Samuel – @juliasamuelmbe
Sibling Loss – @sibling.loss
Sketches from the Cave – @sketchesfromthecave
Untangle Grief – @untanglegrief
What's Your Grief – @whatsyourgrief

Podcasts

Bereavement Room (Callsuma Ali, https://podcasts.apple.com/gb/podcast/bereavement-room/id1488982564)

Dead Parent Club (Kathryn Hooker, Emma Jones, https://deadparentclub.co.uk)

The Full Stop Podcast (for people tackling the disenfranchised grief of involuntary childlessness) (Michael Hughes, Sarah Lawrence and Berenice Smith, https://www.thefullstoppod.com)

Good Mourning (Sally Douglas, Imogen Carn, (https://www.goodmourning.com.au/#1)

Grief Encounters (Ventia Quick, Sasha Hamrogue, https://podcasts.apple.com/ie/podcast/grief-encounters/id1446606717)

Grief Gang (Amber Jeffrey, https://podcasts.apple.com/gb/podcast/the-grief-gang/id1489821860)T

Grief Works (Julia Samuel, https://juliasamuel.co.uk/podcasts/grief-works)

How is Today? (Alby Shale, Clemmie Clough: https://www.howistoday.com/#Podcast)

Terrible, Thanks for Asking (Nora McInerny, https://www.ttfa.org)

What's Your Grief? (Eleanor Haley, Litsa Willams, https://podcasts.apple.com/us/podcast/whats-your-grief-podcast-grief-support-for-those-who/id946757971)

Twitter
Young Orphans @youngorphans

Websites
The Dinner Party (https://www.thedinnerparty.org)
Modern Loss (https://modernloss.com)
Refuge in Grief (https://refugeingrief.com)
What's Your Grief (https://whatsyourgrief.com)

Advance Care Planning
Dementia UK – https://www.dementiauk.org/get-support/
legal-and-financial-information/advance-care-plann
ing/#what
Marie Curie – https://www.mariecurie.org.uk/help/support/
terminal-illness/planning-ahead/advance-care-planning
NHS End of Life Care – https://www.nhs.uk/conditions/
end-of-life-care

Notes

CHAPTER 1
'most people do not grieve in stages' – Margaret Stroebe, Henk Schut and Kathrin Boerner, 'Cautioning Health-Care Professionals: Bereaved Persons Are Misguided Through the Stages of Grief', *Omega*, Vol. 74, Issue 4, 1 March 2017.

CHAPTER 2
'[Dickens] wanted to be "buried in an inexpensive, unostentatious ...' – https://theconversation.com/charles-dickens-newly-discovered-documents-reveal-truth-about-his-death-and-burial-130079.
'For children, if above ten years old ...' – 'By A Lady', *The Workwoman's Guide, containing instructions to the inexperienced in cutting out and completing those articles of wearing apparel, &c ...*, Simpkin Marshall & Co., 1840, p. 122.

CHAPTER 3
'Dr Sofka cites an example in the United States ...' – https://socialworkpodcast.blogspot.com/2017/02/digital-death.html.

'In 2011, a UK internet troll ... ' – https://
www.theguardian.com/uk/2011/sep/13/inter
net-troll-jailed-mocking-teenagers.
'In the 2012 case, the mother of a fifteen-year-old girl ...'
  – https://mashable.com/article/facebook-memori
als-can-be-improved/?europe=true#BHU1sSO8caqx.
'The parents then appealed ... ' – https://www.bbc.
co.uk/news/world-europe-44804599.
'... legacy contact service ...' – https://www.
independent.co.uk/life-style/social-media-what-happ
ens-when-you-die-instagram-facebook-twitter-gmail-
pinterest-a8706126.html.
'It is easier to let information accumulate ... ' – Viktor
Mayer-Schönberger quoted in C. J. Sofka, I. N. Cupit,
and K. R. Gilbert (eds), *Dying, Death, and Grief in an
Online Universe: For Counselors and Educators*, Springer,
2011 (kindle edition), p. 5.
'A Twitter post showing iPads ... ' – https://
twitter.com/roto_tudor/status/1334534101265682
434?s=20.

CHAPTER 4

'And the past is the past ...' – C. S. Lewis, *A Grief
Observed*, Faber and Faber Ltd, first published 1961;
Kindle edition, 2014.
a 'yearning and longing for the person ... ' – *What We've
Learnt About Grief*, BBC Radio 4, broadcast 4 April 2021.
'As we adapt ...' – ibid.
'The core, cardinal symptom of PGD ... ' – ibid.

[Robert Webb] 'You couldn't really imagine ... '
– https://play.acast.com/s/griefcast/ep.14rob
ertwebb.

'eminent orphans'; 'one study'; 'that there is only one
kind of response to something terrible ...' – Malcolm
Gladwell, *David and Goliath: Underdogs, Misfits and the Art
of Battling Giants*, Penguin, 2013 (Kindle edition).

CHAPTER 8
'... a BBC video that has been shared ...' – 'BBC
Stories: Like Minds on BBC iPlayer': https://www.c
facebook.com/bbciplayer/videos/2168915343327846.
'... Lauren Herschel, a griefster herself, shared it on
    Twitter...'–https://www.nzherald.co.nz/lifestyle/
    the-ball-and-the-box-woman-goes-viral-with-perf
    ect-explanation-of-the-stages-of-grief/AX72XBB
    7VY2Z66I2FC7JLDCIHI.

Acknowledgements

This book would not have been possible without my podcast, *Griefcast*, which wouldn't have existed without the incredible collection of people who decided to – bravely, honestly and kindly – share their grief stories, from which I have quoted here. Thank you to each and every one of them, and to remembering the people they have lost along the way. I am forever grateful to be able to hear their stories and the echoes of those who are no longer with us. Thank you to the listeners of *Griefcast* for choosing to open their ears to a show about death and grief. Thank you for your support, kindness, expertise, advice and knowledge. The griefsters are a truly special club and one I am very proud to champion.

Griefcast became possible thanks to Kate Holland, my editor, lifesaver, tech expert and sounding board. Without your knowledge and faith, it wouldn't have happened. Thank you to Whistledown Studios as well, where my recordings found a home and one in which my guests and I felt safe enough to share our stories.

Thank you to my literary agent, Nelle, who believed, encouraged, supported, cajoled, told off, supported and listened in exactly the right percentages, every step of the way. To my editor, Alexis, who trusted in me and fought for this book with such passion, right from the start, herding it over every bump a global pandemic could throw in its way. To everyone at Bloomsbury for their unwavering goodwill, compassion and dedication; I feel very lucky to have been on board your ship. To my copy editor Kate, whose patience and empathy with both myself and the book were gratefully received. Thank you to my agents at Independent Talent, Sarah and Humphrey, for their encouragement as I disappeared into my writing hole.

Thank you to the professionals who gave me their time and expertise, Julia Samuel, Dr Kathryn Mannix, Kimberley St John, Sam Lock, Anna Lyons, Dr Irene Casey and Professor Mark Taubert.

Thank you to Sara, for being my best friend and my book-journey friend. If you hadn't gone there before me, I would have been very lost. Thank you for always showing me the way.

Thank you to my mum, I am so grateful for your love, acceptance, and the joy you managed to bring to us on our grief journey. We wouldn't have made it without you.

Thank you to my brother Tom and the Lloyd-Nuts. I couldn't have wished for a better big brother to face this with. He would have been so astonishingly proud of you and them.

Thank you to my incredible children, he would have loved you so much – which is heart-breaking some days but mostly a reminder that I'm the luckiest mum to have met you both. You are my world.

And lastly, but never leastly: to my husband Ben. This book is here because of you. As I am most days. I couldn't have done this without you – and I know you'll say that's not true but there's a truth to it. Mothers can't write unless someone else holds them up. You have held me up, held my hand, held this house, our children, our lives, all of it together. Sorry it took so long. (I blame the new baby and the pandemic.) Thank you so much for everything.

A Note on the Author

Cariad Lloyd is an actor, comedian, improviser, podcaster and writer. She is the creator and host of the award-winning podcast *Griefcast*, where she talks to people about their experiences of grief and death. Past guests have included Adam Buxton, Jimmy Carr, Sara Pascoe, David Baddiel, Isabel Allende, Fleur East, Monty Don, Fi Glover and Nish Kumar. It won Podcast of the Year at the British Podcast Awards in 2018. Cariad has also appeared in *Peep Show, Have I Got News For You and QI*, and is one of the creators of the hit improv show, *Austentatious*.

A Note on the Type

The text of this book is set in Perpetua. This typeface is an adaptation of a style of letter that had been popularised for monumental work in stone by Eric Gill. Large scale drawings by Gill were given to Charles Malin, a Parisian punch-cutter, and his hand-cut punches were the basis for the font issued by Monotype. First used in a private translation called 'The Passion of Perpetua and Felicity', the italic was originally called Felicity.